T

Preston Tucker was a man with a vision of the "car of tomorrow," and he created it in the late 1940s!

CAR ENGINES OF ALUMINUM COMING SOON, said a headline in late 1958, followed by a story on General Motors. GM spokesmen said the engine would weigh up to 200 pounds less, reducing the weight throughout the entire car, including the chassis, tires and brakes, and improving weight distribution. The Tucker aluminum engine had been designed ten years before!

Rear engine? Individual suspension? Air cooling? Tucker had them all—and until the Corvair, it also had the only true airplane-type engine among the many that had been so publicized. An early brochure illustrated swivel front seats. (Standard seats were used in first models because they were cheaper and easier to get.) Torsion springing? Tucker had it. In addition, a padded dash was a Tucker first.

The company applied for patents on a steering wheel that would retract in a crash . . . and another patent was for a speedometer that would warn the driver, both visually and audibly, when any given speed was exceeded. . . .

Speed? There are stock Tuckers on the road today that will do well over 100 without even breathing hard. . . .

THE INDOMITABLE
TIN GOOSE

PRESTON TUCKER
A Biography

CHARLES T. PEARSON

POCKET BOOKS

New York   London   Toronto   Sydney   Tokyo

Originally published as *The Indomitable Tin Goose: The True Story of Preston Tucker and His Car.*

Quotations from "What About Mr. Tucker and his Dream Car?" by Ken W. Purdy, originally published in *True,* and "We Drive and Test the New Tucker Car" by Tom McCahill, originally published in *Mechanix Illustrated,* are reprinted by permission of Fawcett Publications, Inc.

POCKET BOOKS, a division of Simon & Schuster Inc.
1230 Avenue of the Americas, New York, N.Y. 10020

Published by arrangement with Harper & Row Publishers Inc.
Library of Congress Catalog Card Number: 60-7214

ISBN: 0-671-66046-2

First Pocket Books printing August 1988

10 9 8 7 6 5 4 3 2 1

POCKET and colophon are trademarks of
Simon & Schuster Inc.

Printed in the U.S.A.

If the Golden Chariots in the Hereafter have internal combustion engines, Preston Tucker by now will have designs at least six milleniums ahead of current models. If there is compassion in the Hereafter, he will build them.

Contents

Part Three Behind the Headlines

Foreword

Preston Tucker was beyond question one of the most controversial figures of the late 1940s, and mention of the Tucker automobile can still start arguments that are as far from being settled as they were twelve years ago.

A writer of fiction might be tempted to weave the story of Tucker and his automobile into a novel. But the facts are more fantastic than any fictional version could possibly be.

Discussion of Tucker usually involves, with variations, three basic questions:

Did Tucker actually intend to build a car, or was he just another con man?

Was it any good?

What really happened?

This book, within the limits of space and readability, will try to answer these questions.

Part One

Crazy for Cars

1

Ten Years Ahead
of Tomorrow

SINCE ADVERTISING DEVELOPED FIXED FORMULAS AND NOT so hidden persuaders, one of the most reliable techniques for selling automobiles has been fashioned around the magic word, "Tomorrow."

The theory behind the Tomorrow motif probably is that the American public has been conditioned to expect that everything it enjoys today will be hopelessly obsolete tomorrow, so that any product which even hints of tomorrow must at once become highly desirable. The words change but the theme is constant: The Car of Tomorrow—Tomorrow's Car Today!

In more than twenty years, from the early 1930s until late in 1959, only one new automobile designed for mass production has, by the record, fulfilled its promise of being the "car of tomorrow," and that is the Tucker 48. Now, more than ten years after Preston Tucker flashed briefly across world headlines, features of the Tucker have been adopted one after another by major auto companies. And other features, pioneered by Tucker, are announced impressively as new developments still to come.

Was Tucker actually ten years ahead? The record says the industry hasn't caught up yet. Tucker was a man with an obsession; he had a vision of the "car of tomorrow," and he had it in the late 1940s.

"Car Engines of Aluminum Coming Soon," said a headline late in 1958, followed by a story on General Motors, warning the iron industry to be prepared for a switch from iron to aluminum engines. GM spokesmen said the engine would weigh up to 200 pounds less, reducing weight throughout the entire car, including the chassis, tires and brakes, and improving weight distribution. The Tucker engine was aluminum ten years ago.

Rear engine? Individual suspension? Air-cooling? Tucker had them all—and until the Corvair, it also had the only true airplane-type engine among the many that had been so publicized. An early brochure illustrated swivel front seats. (Standard seats were used in first models because they were cheaper and easier to get.) Torsion springing? Tucker had it. Not perfect, but few new features are perfect the first time 'round. In addition, the padded dash was a Tucker first.

The company had applied for patents on a steering wheel which would retract in a crash, instead of impaling or crushing the driver's chest, and another patent was for a speedometer that would warn the driver, both visually and audibly, when any given speed was exceeded. Tucker wanted 13-inch wheels before the industry had 14, and announced a 24-volt electrical system before the industry changed to 12.

Popularity of Tucker features was still evident in 1957 when the Cadillac "75" had doors that opened into the roof. The year before, the Cornell Aeronautical Laboratories at Buffalo built a model "Safety Car" which included Tucker's padded dash, a curved front bumper to deflect blows instead of taking them head on, and a single driver's seat in the center. Tucker had announced all three more than ten years before.

A highly publicized feature in one '59 model was a tread five inches wider; the Tucker rear tread was five inches wider in 1947. Use of automatic transmissions increased from 25.4 per cent in 1949 to 74 per cent in 1956, with the curve rising rapidly in 1959. Tucker was already tooling for 100 per cent automatic transmissions, reached by Cadillac in 1953, five years later. Speed? There are stock Tuckers on the road today that will do well over 100 without even breathing hard—and on regular gasoline, which wasn't even considered a selling point by anybody important until 1959.

Inevitably the question will be asked: "If the Tucker was so good and so far ahead, why wasn't it built?"

Many answers were advanced at the time, many with convincing evidence to support them. Among the answers:

Tucker was his own worst enemy, and was responsible himself for most of his troubles.

The automotive industry knocked him down to eliminate dangerous competition, working through officials high in government.

Persons tried to convict Tucker to further their own political ambitions.

Or was it only an unfortunate mistake in timing, plunging in the colorful tradition of Ford and Durant and Chrysler, in an era when plunging had gone out of fashion?

The answer is somewhere in the record, but even after the story is told the truth may still be elusive. It may be that Tucker's story is important for only one reason—that it dramatized the end of an era of speculative investment which had brought progress beyond man's wildest dreams, an era which already had changed to an age interested only in security.

Many people remember the fabulous Tin Goose but few, even at the time, knew the circumstances of its birth, or realized the complexity of intrigue which ended its short but spectacular career.

It was in 1944 that I first met Preston Tucker. I was covering the automotive beat for United Press in Detroit. The town was buzzing with rumors. Who would be the first to get back into production with a postwar dream car? What would it be like?

Henry Ford II was dashing over the country making speeches. Maybe in Cleveland they were planning a three-cylinder radial engine in the trunk, while in Baltimore it might be a V-8, or maybe an engine placed crossways in the middle. Automotive writers in Detroit knew Ford was either sending up trial balloons, or just plain having fun and stirring up excitement. They knew the first postwar Fords would be so close to the last 42s that it would be hard to tell the difference. But at the desk at United Press headquarters in New York, they went crazy.

"Need Ford Folo Soonest," they telegraphed, refusing to believe that Henry II was romancing, and that he didn't expect to be taken seriously.

Charles E. Wilson, then president of General Motors, held press conferences in which he flew into huge rages under skillful needling by reporters. He would almost turn purple, and then burst out with a story which GM probably wouldn't otherwise have released for weeks or months. Still, it was about the only usable copy that came out of GM at the time. An approach through regular channels usually ended weeks later in the office of a third vice president, and by the time a story could be cleared it would be dead anyway.

A purely personal problem was that I had a tough man to follow in the job. My immediate predecessor had been Anthony G. (Tony) De Lorenzo, later a vice president of GM, a clean, fast writer who rated tops among the big wheels of United Press in New York and Chicago. De Lorenzo was further esteemed for having Harry Bennett fenced off out at Ford, where he constantly got exclusives that other automotive writers never got close to.

The biggest annoyance to automotive writers was the Fisher brothers, who up to that time had been the softest touch in the entire history of public relations. All they wanted was *not* to get into the papers. So all their head PR man had to do was to go in once a month or so with an armful of newspapers and magazines and say:

"See you weren't in this or this or this," and the brothers would beam happily.

But even the Fishers contracted the fever. They were beginning to sound off too, though it was obvious they were badly out of practice. In self-defense I launched a one-man campaign to smoke out the Fisher brothers, writing a continuous series of nasty stories that somebody, sooner or later, would have to answer. The campaign finally paid off with a press conference in the luxurious tower offices in the Fisher Building.

"We don't know what we're going to do yet," one of the brothers said, "but it'll be something big."

This was the background with an auto-hungry public avid for news, when Ray Russell, a Detroit engineer and one of my best listening posts, suggested:

"Why don't you go and see Tucker? I hear he's got something."

I called Tucker, made an appointment, and drove out a few days later to Ypsilanti, the town where he lived. Tucker received me in his office and practically the first thing he said was that he was developing a completely new design for a car. He dropped this bombshell quietly, explaining that he couldn't say much right now and asking me to keep in touch with him, since he hoped to have something more definite within a few months.

At first sight he was the typical small manufacturer so common around Detroit—well groomed, outwardly prosperous and self-assured. He talked readily and easily, but with reserve, in the manner of a man who commanded attention and expected it. From time to time he would refer to something important he had to hold back now but would reveal when the right time came. I caught no suggestion of the fanatic, yet in the animation of his expression, and the intensity of his brown eyes, I found the promise of a man who was going somewhere. Tucker acted as though he had something that would revolutionize the automobile industry, and his enthusiasm was contagious.

At the time he maintained offices in a large two-story building back of his home, with a small shop space on the ground floor, offices along one side and drafting rooms on the second floor. It was so crowded people were stumbling over each other. In a large metal building about a block away he had a lot of heavy machining equipment and a fairly large force turning out some kind of military equipment which, as was usual at the time, was very hush-hush.

On my next visit to Ypsilanti some months later, he gave me considerably more information, showing me working drawings, sketches and an assortment of parts that later served as props in preliminary stages of his campaign to get backing. The assortment included cast aluminum suspension arms, blocks and heads of Miller engines and related parts.

17

Tucker invited me to stay for dinner. I met his wife and some of the kids who wandered in and out. Dinner was informal with only a suggestion of the hysteria I later found was normal around Tucker. Mrs. Tucker was relaxed, friendly and informal, a mother of five children, a superlative cook and practiced hostess. Of medium height with brown hair, she impressed me as an unfailingly efficient woman who could handle a busy husband and a flock of demanding children with calm dispatch. The dinner couldn't have been better— man's fare, with the accent on meat and potatoes—and I knew that good food had its place in Preston Tucker's affections, together with family and automobiles.

After dinner Tucker and I went to his den, which featured easy chairs and a fireplace, and returned to automobile talk. He didn't have any printed literature, but asked me to see two of his associates in Detroit, who had a large brochure in color in their offices near the General Motors Building. I talked with them and saw the brochure, which told a pretty impressive story. But Tucker still asked me to keep it under wraps for the present, saying he had various deals in progress and didn't want to break it prematurely. I sensed then the superlative drive and daring of the man.

"There's one deal with a plane company that looks like it's just about ready to go," Tucker said. "If the story gets out now it might kill the deal. Even if this one doesn't go I've got others on the fire, and sooner or later we'll get it off the ground. But the deal has to be right."

I told Tucker I would keep it under wraps until he was ready.

Tucker's story interested me just as it was later to interest countless thousands of people in a dozen or more languages. So after I left United Press I called him occasionally to see what progress he might be making, even though I was no longer looking for automotive copy. A year or so later I left a public relations job with a Detroit advertising agency to free lance full time and again was looking for stories, so I continued to keep in touch with Tucker.

In the summer of 1945 he said he was ready. He called me in and I wrote the story, which featured an illustration in color done by an artist working for him at the time. The picture spelled "S-P-E-E-D," even standing still. There were

18

some photographs of parts, a few simple line drawings I did and others done by an artist I had worked with in the agency— Mike Such, now in Hollywood. The story was bought by *Pic,* which scheduled it for January, 1946. To supplement the check from *Pic* I sold rewrites to various science and auto- motive magazines that wouldn't jump *Pic's* release date, and didn't compete in its field. Purely as an accommodation to Tucker, I also wrote press releases for newspapers when the *Pic* story hit the newsstands in December.

At that time, all over the country, people and companies were trying to get into production of new items, or whatever they had been making before the war. Some parts and ser- vices were impossible to get and most of them were in short supply. Raw materials, patterns, castings, machining—every- body was having a rough time.

So when I wrote "off the drawing board into the production stage" high in the first paragraph I assumed, by the time the story was published some months later, that Tucker would have the castings and other stuff he said had been ordered. Many of the stories I was handling at the time followed the same pattern—as soon as they got parts and materials they were in business, and the situation was getting steadily better. When I finally realized there weren't any castings or even patterns I was at first resentful, but later had to admit that, from Tucker's standpoint, there was nothing either dishonest or immoral at the time in referring to something that was still on paper as fact. In the years that followed I learned that to the irrepressible Tucker, with his boundless optimism and self-confidence, anything he had decided to do was already a fact, for all practical purposes, and there was no point in complicating things with a lot of tiresome detail and expla- nations.

In the months that followed, Tucker called me occasionally to help him out with press releases and publicity, covering my expenses for trips to Chicago, Washington and New York. It became a choice between giving up free lancing or desert- ing Tucker. He made me a good offer but laid it on the line: if he won, I would win, and if he lost I couldn't expect to more than break even, if that. I like long shots myself, and further, I felt a personal obligation to do whatever I could to make a reality of the fantastically ambitious promotion that I had inadvertently launched.

Almost a year passed before I fully realized the excitement I had stirred up with my *Pic* story. I had asked the magazine to forward any inquiries direct to Tucker, and the forwarded letters threatened to overflow his office. Tucker said that more than 150,000 letters and telegrams had been received.

On the strength of this response, Tucker threw his campaign into high gear. He had been working quietly more than two years trying to get private financing for a car that was still (as I learned later) largely on paper. He had his faults, as I was to learn, but they were more than counterbalanced by his good qualities, which included genuine enthusiasm, tolerance, belief in himself and the future, and a thirst for knowledge that never faded.

What I found was a man who by his abilities, his vision, his determination, his self-confidence was destined vitally to affect the whole history of automotive design. He knew what he wanted and what the public wanted. That he had shortcomings could be taken for granted. But that he had the right sort of imagination there could be no question. He was the type of man about whom myths collected. These myths would grow and become misinterpreted but they would not be easily forgotten.

2

The Most Talked-About
Car in the World

THAT'S WHAT THE FIRST BROCHURE SAID ON THE COVER: "The Most Talked-About Automobile in the World Today." And it wasn't exaggerating.

Many automobiles have been called "sweethearts" by enthusiastic owners and hysterical copy writers, but no other automobile in history got as many mash notes as the Tucker. By automobile standards any car that has passed its fifth birthday is an old bat, with aging features that makeup can't renew. But ten years later the Tucker was still getting letters from affectionate owners, though some admitted a bit wistfully that they would like to see a new model.

It was truly a *liebeswagen,* and a Tucker on the street even today can still stop traffic and excite the admiration of kids who never heard of its maker. An owner in California wrote: "We are constantly being followed or stopped on the road to be plied with questions. Are they being built now? Where can one be ordered from? They think that ours is brand new."

Some of the features, which almost overnight captured the world's imagination, may have been idealistic and at the time impractical, or would have needed years of research and development. But enough of those features were retained to satisfy the public, which had learned through long, sad experience that few sweethearts ever meet the promise of first infatuation.

The first story started the *affaire*. "Designed to cruise continuously at 100 miles per hour, the new 150-horsepower Tucker 'Torpedo' is powered by an airplane-type engine of entirely new design . . . flat with opposed cylinders, largely aluminum, that can be taken out and replaced in 30 minutes," the story said. No American stock car had yet reached that horsepower.

The name "Torpedo" was dropped after it was decided to emphasize safety rather than speed.

"It has a 126-inch wheelbase . . . the front tread is standard and the rear tread two inches wider for greater stability. Front fenders turn with the wheels, and driving lights on the fenders follow curves in the road. A single 'Cyclops Eye' fixed center light completes the headlight assembly, all to be controlled by a photoelectric cell that automatically dims the lights when meeting another car. Interior upholstery will be durable, fadeless, washable plastic or other synthetic fabric." It would have a low center of gravity, road balance and independent wheel suspension that "will eliminate weaving at high speeds, and creeping on curves."

Early press releases and literature followed the original story, featuring disc brakes, fuel injection and one item that was too much even for Tucker, who said he would have a torque converter design "that eliminates clutch, transmission, drive shaft and torque tube, differential and differential housing with an estimated saving in weight of 600 to 800 pounds."

"The driver's seat is in the center, with the first real provision for seeing out since dashboards were given back to the carriage makers. But Tucker isn't going to be obstinate about it—if people insist on having the steering wheel at the left where they're used to it, he can move it back. Seats on either side of the driver swivel out of the way when the doors are opened. The windshield is a single piece of curved safety glass without obstructing corner posts or center upright. The doors will open into the roof so it won't be necessary to stoop getting in."

"Tucker has an extensive background in the designing and building of racing cars," another release stated, "and was associated with the late Harry Miller, whose cars won 14 out of 16 races at the Indianapolis Speedway." Publicity men talked of "a price around $1,000." However, that was a goal and those who knew prices and that costs of parts and labor were rising knew that the final price would be much higher than that. But such a price appealed to the imagination; it led to the belief that a reasonable price could be expected.

Tucker's aggressive announcements already were arousing fear in Detroit that he might become a threat to established manufacturers. After all, the right kind of salesmanship can sell almost anything and most people agreed that Tucker had that magic touch.

"Like his car, Preston Tucker is a bit on the spectacular side," wrote one reporter, "a well built, well dressed man with a genial face and a gregarious personality." One magazine called him a "personable, rather handsome 45-year-old Michigander with a gift for mile-a-minute talk and a flair for vivid bow ties and white socks." Another description was "Boyish, bow-tied Tucker," which persisted until in self-defense he gave away every bow tie he owned. The Tucker car was in comic strips; some sorority girls voted him "the man they'd most like to be marooned with on a desert island," and the Tucker car became a standard gag on radio shows.

People could not account for it specifically, but Tucker represented a dream come true of a young American boy who had caught the popular imagination. Without knowing anything about the car itself, people could envisage an ideal car, designed by an ideal-looking young man, selling to the popular market.

Six feet tall and almost always well dressed, Tucker made an excellent appearance and he was equally at home speaking to a group from a platform, or in his office. He had a heavy frame but was never fat, and he never weighed more than 200 pounds. Men found him convincing, and most women thought he was handsome. Except for his ties, he dressed conservatively, and he invariably bought the best in clothes.

In spite of his reputation as a super-salesman, Tucker was not overly articulate. He felt keenly his lack of facility with words, and he often wrote or dictated endless pages trying to express himself outside the only subject he really knew— automobiles. While he finished high school and spent some time at Cass Technical School in Detroit, he never went to college, and this very lack of formal education became an asset. He looked like a college man without being one, a fact that could be admired. He was a malapropist, but that often contributed to his wit, for his grammatical errors weren't a pose. When he said "exhilarate" for "accelerate" he may have been unconsciously expressing his feeling for automobiles better than if he had used the right word. His daughter Marilyn once said:

"I tried to get Daddy to say 'fiscal year' instead of talking about the 'physical year' as he always did. And he said, 'They know what I'm talking about,' and I had to admit he had a point."

Grammar was the least of his worries. His mind concentrated on other things. Once he began talking he showed an actor's instinct for catching the mood of his audience. After a few tries, we never wrote his speeches for him. Occasionally he would use notes, but most of the time he just talked off the cuff and when he lacked specific information he improvised, and effectively. If he sometimes manhandled the immediate facts, his purpose was to instill in his listeners the same enthusiasm and confidence that he felt himself. Because Tucker never doubted that ultimately he would make the facts suit his own purposes.

There can be no question that Tucker was something of a visionary, or that he was asking for trouble when he proposed actually to do things that others in the field only talked about, or flatly condemned as impossible. Anybody who sticks his head above the crowd automatically invites somebody to knock it off. Quite likely the guy who invented the wheel had to dodge a lot of big rocks in his day, rocks thrown by people who believed that if wheels were practical the big tribes would already have them.

From early childhood Tucker had one interest in life, and one loyalty, that came ahead of family, friends and security. Loyalty to his conception of automotive design, along with an unshakable determination to build automobiles, was his one central item of integrity and he never lost it. Building an automobile that came as close as was humanly possible to his ideal was perhaps the one moral obligation Tucker recognized.

The romance between the public and the Tucker car was nothing more than an extension of Tucker's own lifelong love affair with automobiles, which had started on a brilliant summer day in the country in Michigan when he was six years old.

Preston was visiting his grandfather that summer of 1909, but his mind was not on nature or matters agricultural. Unlike most kids, he never cared a hoot for country life.

He was out on the country road riding with his grandfather in a buggy behind a team of horses. It was a dusty, gravel road in northern Michigan. Suddenly they heard a car coming. Grandfather stopped the horses, jumped out of the buggy and grabbed the reins up close. This was standard, conventional practice in those days before horses had become accustomed to cars. He hollered to the boy to jump out too. "That fool with his gasoline buggy may scare the horses," the old gentleman explained. "We have to hold them so they won't run away."

To Preston this was an unforgettable experience. He did not sympathize with the horses or feel sorry for the old man. His mind was hypnotized by the car he saw coming. It was sort of weaving along the rough road. About half a block away the car stopped and the driver motioned to Grandfather to lead the horses past.

When the animals smelled gasoline they shied and reared, but Grandfather got them past the car and tied them to a tree beside the road. Then he walked over to speak to the driver, who was a doctor from his town.

Preston's eyes could not leave the car. The gasoline smell that scared the horses and made his grandfather swear was perfume to him. Preston had seen pictures of automobiles but this was the first time he had actually seen one. It was almost like a religious conversion. What the boy had seen was a vision, a symbolic sign of his own future, an experience he would never forget.

Almost in a daze, too excited to ask questions, Preston got

back into his grandfather's buggy and went down the road. He looked back at the shiny red automobile. It grew smaller, but he promised himself that he would own a car like that some day. Soon afterward he was examining designs and determining to build a car of his own that everyone else would admire.

This incident was the inspiration of Preston's early life. As he looked back it seemed to him the only experience he could remember. Much of the story of his early life was told to me by his mother, Mrs. Lucille Holmes, who remarried in 1928 after the death of her first husband in 1905.

Mrs. Holmes was never an easygoing person. Determined and self-reliant, she had experienced hardship and poverty, and she was a complete realist in appraising the world and its difficulties. When she talked of Preston she was at times surprisingly objective, not the usual doting mother to whom a favorite son could do no wrong. From the first meeting you knew she could not be changed or pushed around. She demanded respect and she expected obedience.

Unquestionably Preston inherited from her much of that determination that characterized him all his life. From that moment when, as a boy, he saw his first automobile he achieved a purpose in life and he never deviated from it. His ambition became fixed and it carried him through every obstacle, even to his last days.

3

Wheels in His Heart

PRESTON THOMAS TUCKER WAS BORN SEPTEMBER 21, 1903, at Capac, Michigan, a small town not far from Port Huron. His grandfather ran a plant that made briquettes from the sod in nearby peat swamps and his father, Shirl Tucker, worked in the plant. His mother was just 21 years old, and had married at 19. A second son, William, was born two years later.

"I guess Preston took after his father," said his mother, later Mrs. Holmes. "Before we moved to Capac, Shirl worked on the railroad at Boyne City hauling out logs. He was mechanically inclined and he was crazy about that railroad."

When Preston was two years old his father died, following an attack of appendicitis. That left his mother with two small boys to support, her only resources being her own strong will and a provisional teaching certificate from Ferris Institute at Big Rapids, Michigan.

"I started teaching in a country school in Osceola County," she said. "And I kept on teaching until the First World War.

Then my sister, Harriet, who was working in Detroit, wanted me to come there. My sister said I could do better. So I took all my furniture and we moved into a house at Ecorse Road and Fort Street, what is now Lincoln Park. I worked in an office for a while but I didn't like it so I went back to teaching. That meant I had to go to summer school every year to keep up my certificate.

"I worked all the time and it was really kind of funny. I had certain rules that the kids had to be home for meals and be in before dark. Where they were in the daytime when they weren't in school I didn't know, but at nights they were home unless they had permission to go somewhere. I would walk right into a poolroom and take them out. I didn't fool.

"They were pretty good kids, both of them, and about the only trouble I had was Preston always getting his clothes all full of grease and dirt, hanging around garages and used car lots. I used to say, 'How do you think I'm going to keep you clean for school?'

"Keeping him clean was the biggest problem—but Preston thought he was doing something worthwhile and I guess in a way he was. He was never lazy, he was always doing something. Maybe they only paid him a quarter for running errands or helping, but he was never any trouble. When other kids were out playing he was working and learning everything he could from mechanics and car salesmen.

"They both had to have bicycles, of course, and I guess Preston was sixteen when he coaxed me to get our first car. It was an Overland touring and Preston made the deal himself. I think the man's name was White and we gave him $300. It was a good car, shiny, and it looked good and ran good. We had it a year and a half, and then Preston sold it for $300, and he got cash. Next we had a Model T coupe. It cost $300, too, but there was something wrong with it. I told him, 'Preston, you'd better sell it,' and he did, for $350.

"A few weeks later he got a big Chandler touring car. The man wanted $750 but Preston said, 'I'll give you $350.' That was all the money he had and the man took it. I told him, 'You've got to sell it, that car is too big for us.' But by now Preston thought he was quite a mechanic and he said it needed a little fixing before he could sell it. I came home from school one day and there were gears and things all over the garage floor, with numbers on the floor in chalk.

"I said to him, 'What in the world are you doing?' He said he was fixing the transmission. I said, 'You'll never get it back together again,' and he said, 'I will too. I know just how I took the parts out and I've got them all numbered.'

"We finally had to pay a mechanic $64 to get it back together, and I told Preston again, 'I don't want that big car,' so he sold it for $610. Next he bought a 'Harroun,' I think it was. Ray Harroun, a fellow who had some money, started making them in Wayne, and Preston said they were fast and snappy and just what he wanted. He was going to Cass Technical school in Detroit and driving the car to school.

"I told him, 'You know what's going to happen? Some day that car is going to stop right in the middle of the street and you'll never get it started again, and I don't care.' And that was just what happened. That was the end of that car and it was the only one we ever lost money on, but it didn't cost very much to start with. All the time he went to school he worked. For a while he worked in a soda fountain in Detroit, and later he was an office boy at Cadillac."

At Cadillac he was office boy for D. McCall White, one of the top officials, and while there he developed a new technique to expedite his work. Young Tucker made his rounds on roller skates, delivering messages and memorandums with spectacular speed. One day when he skidded around a corner he whammed right square into White, which probably shortened his career at Cadillac, as he left shortly after. Many laughed about this, but Preston was serious; he was concentrating on speed and efficiency.

Tucker was growing up with the lusty new automobile industry, and his idols were the men who drove the thundering monsters that roared around the new track at Indianapolis, where speeds already had passed 100 miles an hour. It was a new era of giants, both men and machines, names that have been engraved indelibly in the history of man's progress toward ever increasing speed, and Preston Tucker dreamed of the day when he could join the pioneers who were making automotive history.

In the early days at Indianapolis almost all the major companies entered cars in the race, and their names are remembered today with reverence by people who love automobiles. Marmon, Duesenberg, Stutz, Mercer, Apperson, Lozier, Simplex and Velie. Driving on the Buick race team were the three Chevrolet brothers, Gaston, Louis and Arthur. It was Art Chevrolet who later worked for Tucker in Ypsilanti and New Orleans. From Europe came Isotta-Fraschini, Opel, Fiat, Sunbeam, Peugeot and Bugatti, and the big German Benz driven by Barney Oldfield. Ralph DePalma was there, and Eddie Rickenbacker, both of whom Tucker later came to know intimately. In 1920 Gaston Chevrolet drove a Monroe designed and built by his brother Louis, to bring in an American-built automobile as winner for the first time since 1912.

When later in Chicago Tucker brought in men he had known at Indianapolis it wasn't for their prestige that had impressed him as a boy. It was because he knew they were good, and for another reason—he planned one day to build up his own racing team to challenge the road racing champions of Europe, and bring the trophies back to his own country.

But all that was still far in the future. His prized Harroun had let him down, and he had to keep working to help his mother out at home and get money ahead to buy another automobile.

"Preston was pretty good giving money to me," said his mother. "Both the boys were always good that way. When his friends were out of work Preston always had a job, and the only one I didn't like was when he started working for the police in Lincoln Park."

It wasn't police work that attracted young Tucker as much as the chance to ride motorcycles and drive squad cars on special jobs, like running errands and parades, when they needed extras.

"If I got him off that police force once I must have done it a dozen times," his mother said. "It was pretty wild and woolly around there then and I was always afraid there would be shooting. After he got married there wasn't much I could do about it because he needed the job to support a family."

In the summer when he was eighteen, Tucker had met Vera Fuqua, a pretty Detroit girl who worked in the telephone office in Detroit. Up to that time, his mother said he never paid much attention to girls, but they soon started going steady and they were married two years later in 1923, when Tucker was twenty. When they met he was working at Ford, operating a machine.

"I didn't like that," his mother said, "and I told him, 'Don't you stand at a machine all day. Make them give you a job where you can learn something.' I think he finally got some kind of a checking job."

Tucker left Ford and went back to the police force, where he was right in the middle of the excitement of Prohibition days. Life with Tucker may have been hectic at times but it was seldom dull, and Vera got a preview one night before they were married when he took her, along with his brother and another girl, to a baseball dance in Lincoln Park.

"Things were wide open," Vera said, recalling the night. "There were a lot of tough characters who didn't like Preston because he worked with the police, and besides his mother had been giving them a lot of trouble trying to stop cock fights in the downriver section.

"It was about midnight when some fellow started waving a $50 bill in the air and yelling that he could lick anybody in the place, and he was looking right at Preston. I said, 'Nobody's going to fight anybody—I'm leaving right now.'

"All four of us ran down the stairs and got in our car—it was an Oakland—and people were popping up around cars all over the place. We started up Fort Street with Preston driving when somebody started shooting at us and two or three cars came after us. They tried to run us off the road, and when that didn't work they tried to pin us between them.

"I kept watching and telling Preston 'left' and 'right' so they couldn't get up alongside of us. We must have been doing sixty or more and we were coming to a bridge over the Rouge River when Preston said, 'I'm going to try something—don't get scared.'

"He let one car get almost even with us and then swerved clear to the left so the other car had to leave the road or run into the side of the bridge. When I looked back it was plowing into the ditch, but the other car was still right behind us.

"Preston kept driving up Fort Street until he got to Grand Boulevard. There he spun the car around in a sharp left turn and drove right up the middle of the parkway to the Scotten Avenue fire station. I guess I wasn't really scared until it was all over."

Tucker first joined the Lincoln Park police force officially in 1922 when he was nineteen. He worked eleven months before his mother stooled on him again, and they had to let him go because he was underage. Floyd Crichton, Lincoln Park Chief of Police, was a rookie in the department too at the time, and says he understood why Tucker's mother objected.

"That two-mile stretch of riverfront along Ecorse was one of the toughest areas in the whole country," he said. "It was a main port of entry for booze from Canada, and more money changed hands there during bootlegging days than anywhere else in the United States. It was a tough district and being a cop was a tough job.

"Pres and I worked together. We rode motorcycles daytimes ten months of the year and squad cars after midnight. Pres was a good cop. There wasn't a damn thing he was afraid of and he could spot a booze runner a mile off. He learned all the tricks of dirty fighting in the police and he could handle a gun. I don't think he ever started a fight, but if he had to he never hesitated.

"In those days they hauled liquor in big touring cars, with the rear springs built up to carry the load. When we saw a car going through town with the rear end riding high we knew they were empty, and when they came back through with the back springs dragging they had a load. The big operators averaged two loads a week, and some loads would bring $3,000 wholesale, retailing up to $10 a gallon. So the boys driving those cars were plenty tough."

The last time Tucker's mother got him booted off the police force, he took over a gas station that was for lease cheap, because a new road was going in and the station had only six months to go. It was a one-man operation, and when he had to go to Detroit or somewhere on business, his young wife took over.

Putting their first daughter Shirley in the baby carriage, Vera wheeled it about eight blocks to the station where she pumped gas and sold oil and accessories until Tucker got back. He didn't really want a service station except for a base to sell automobiles, but the station paid his overhead and what he made selling cars was clear profit. He was in business for himself for the first time, and he traded and sold everything he could get his hands on.

When his six-month lease expired he went back to the police force, and by this time he was twenty-one and there wasn't much his mother could do about it. She was always afraid there would be some shooting and she was right. A faded, torn clipping from a Lincoln Park paper tells of the day he brought in two armed bank robbers singlehanded.

On a Sunday afternoon he was alone driving a big Hudson squad car when he spotted a car that had been reported stolen from Highland Park, a Detroit suburb. The car was an eight-cylinder Peerless touring, and when he forced it to the curb two men in the front seat had him covered with pistols.

"Just keep right on going and you won't get hurt," the driver told him.

Tucker went on, but he circled the block and started after the Peerless with his service revolver in his lap and a sawed-off shotgun on the seat beside him. People ran for the curbs as the Peerless sped through the village with the Hudson behind, siren screaming. A little way outside of town the car in front plowed through a light fence and across a field, with the Hudson right behind. Across the rough field they went, through a wooden fence and back onto the highway.

Through the field and down the highway Tucker drove with his right hand and shot around the windshield with his left, while one of the men in the Peerless shot back. At the end of a straight six-mile stretch the Peerless missed a sharp turn and came skidding and sliding to a stop in the soft mud of a plowed field.

Tucker jumped from the Hudson with his shotgun in one hand and his pistol in the other. He ordered the men to throw down their guns and get out of the car. When they got out he

33

threw them a pair of unlocked handcuffs and told them to handcuff themselves together.

One man said he didn't know how. Tucker thought he was reaching for another gun, so he shot him through a shoulder with his pistol. Then they put the cuffs on, and Tucker ordered them back into the car, where he handcuffed one of the men to the steering wheel.

Then he raised the hood of the Peerless and disconnected four spark plugs to hold its speed down, gathered up the two revolvers and made the men drive the car ahead of him to the police station.

After the men were booked, it turned out that they were brothers who reportedly had robbed a bank in suburban Ferndale a few days earlier. Another brother had escaped from prison in Atlanta and sent word through the grapevine that he was coming to Lincoln Park to get Tucker.

"We put in some anxious days and nights," Mrs. Tucker said. "Preston's grandmother—we called her Ma Preston— was living with us and there were the children. We kept the shades pulled down and every time we heard a car backfire we were scared stiff."

But the third brother never reached Lincoln Park. He was shot and killed trying to hold up a bank in Cleveland.

Automobiles had got Tucker on the police force and automoblies finally got him off. The touring cars of the day had no heaters, and Tucker decided it was silly to freeze with all that heat going to waste under the hood. So he borrowed an acetylene torch from the Department of Public Works, cut a hole through the dash, and piped hot air in from the manifold.

"It was early spring and the DPW was in hot water as usual that time of year," said Crichton. "When it thawed, the streets started breaking up and every time some citizen hit a hole he would raise hell with the DPW. So when some taxpayer heard about Tucker cutting a hole in a city-owned squad car with a DPW torch, he was in trouble. They had no authority to lend the torch, and the next thing that would have happened would have been a hearing on destroying public property."

Although no official action was taken, Tucker was demoted

to walking a beat and while on night patrol he won first prize in a contest he hadn't even known was going on.

Passing a tailor shop with his Doberman pup, which he had taken in on a car deal, he heard voices and shouting inside. The door was locked, so he climbed through the transom to investigate. The shouting was coming from a radio and he was just in time to hear the closing announcement on a prize contest!

"And remember, the person who wires this station tonight from the greatest distance will receive free—absolutely free—an incomparable Oriole Super Heterodyne Radio."

Tucker picked up the phone and called the telegraph office to send a wire to the radio station in St. Louis, and a few days later the Tucker household boasted a brand new radio.

Like most of the radios of that time it had a separate power unit about the size of present automobile batteries, and while Vera was delighted with the radio she flatly refused to have all that wire and junk cluttering up her living room. There was a closet off the room, so Tucker took his service revolver and blasted a hole through the wall for the wires.

"Lots faster than going after a drill," he explained. "Easier, too."

"If it wasn't some kind of machinery or something it was animals," Vera said. "Preston was always bringing home stray dogs and cats. One day he came home for lunch and told me to reach into his pocket. I wouldn't do it, because it could be a squirrel or almost anything.

"He said, 'Don't be afraid, I've got a present for you.' I put my hand in and felt something furry and jumped about ten feet. Then he pulled out a white rat. His name was Pete and he would come when you called him.

"We had just moved into another house and there were mice, and somebody told Preston if there were rats in the house the mice wouldn't stay around. From then on, between the Doberman and Pete, we didn't have any mice.

"The last thing at night we would find Pete and put him in a desk with a hinge top and shut the lid. One night I couldn't find him. I called and called. I was just going to give up and went in to look at Preston Junior, who was a

35

baby then, and there was Pete sound asleep between Preston's legs.

"I grabbed that rat and threw him across the room into the desk and slammed the top down. Pete's tail was sticking out, and from then on it was bent at a forty-five-degree angle. I felt so sorry for that poor rat. But I didn't want him sleeping with the children, so we finally gave him to a little boy in the neighborhood."

Tucker laughed about it. He couldn't help making deals—swapping and trading were too much fun—and he was a born trader. Very soon he would put this instinct to work in the field where he was destined to make his mark.

4

Birth of a Salesman

AFTER THE LEASE ON THE GAS STATION WAS UP AND TUCKER went back to the police force, he began selling Studebakers on the side. During this time he met Mitchell Dulian, who was factory sales manager for Hamtramck and one of the best automobile salesmen in the business, then or since, setting sales records almost everywhere he worked. Short and dark, always conservatively well dressed, he had smooth strong features that baffled anyone trying to guess his age by twenty years, then or now. He thought, talked and most likely dreamed automobiles, which probably was the secret of his success. Shortly after meeting Tucker he needed a salesman, so he called Tucker, who promptly took the job.

Tucker had been selling cars since he wore knee pants, and smoking cigars because he thought it made him look older. But Dulian gave him his first full-time job as a salesman, where he could try out some of his ideas for selling.

Hamtramck at the time was one of the wildest and most colorful sections of Detroit, largely Polish, with a nationwide reputation for bootlegging and gambling. Boisterous wedding parties often lasted for days, and sometimes the polkas turned into fights, with squad cars lined up to haul guests off to the jug to sleep it off. Old-time cab drivers say that on pay days there would be long lines of waiting customers, two abreast, stretching down the streets and around the corners in front of the prosperous bordellos, which ran three eight-hour shifts. The era of mass production was in full bloom.

"Preston Tucker really surprised me as a salesman, and I had been in the business a long time," Dulian said. "Within a few days he started selling cars, and it was only a short time before we outsold every other branch in Detroit. He had the gift of knowing what men wanted and what they would pay.

"His enthusiasm and new ideas were endless. We would have parades of our automobiles ending up on some main corner, where Tucker would go into his sales routine just like an old-time medicine man. He would make friends in the big stores and garages, and have them put up posters for our salesroom. Then he would make a deal with the storekeeper or garageman to send us prospects for a commission, and soon he had bird dogs all over town."

But although Tucker was making more money than he had ever made before in his life, Hamtramck was a long hard drive from Lincoln Park, and he was still just a salesman. He wanted to run his own show. So he left Dulian and went back on the police force for the last time.

But he was just marking time there, because some influential citizens still remembered the stink over cutting holes in the squad car and were just waiting for another chance. Meanwhile, Dulian was transferred to Memphis, where he had two places and needed a manager to handle one of them. He wired Tucker, offering him the job.

"When Preston got that wire I was so tickled I started packing right away," his wife said. "All the time I was expecting Marilyn, our third baby, and Preston's mother was getting things ready for the doctor."

Tucker wired Dulian to expect him the next day. He left without even bothering to resign, and the police department gave him a leave of absence. The action was never rescinded, and technically Tucker was still on leave of absence from the force when he died.

"I drove Preston to the Michigan Central depot and saw him off on the train," Mrs. Tucker said, "and the next day Marilyn was born."

A few months later Dulian's and Tucker's families moved to Memphis. Meanwhile Dulian and Tucker lived at the Claridge Hotel and had to walk through the park going to the automobile agencies. The one Tucker handled was on Union Avenue.

Memphis had many lively characters in the automobile sales business. It also had the laziest squirrels in the world. Preston easily placed himself at the top among the auto salesman and was one of the busiest promoters in town. Yet he also had eyes for animals and especially squirrels. Memphis squirrels are so fat that they almost fall out of trees coming down in the morning for free handouts, and at night they puff and pant climbing back up.

Dulian couldn't understand the parades of squirrels that always followed them through the park until one day he noticed Tucker dropping peanuts as they walked along. But Preston's inner thoughts had not been diverted by the squirrels. He was canvassing the whole automobile-selling field in Memphis, getting a line on how his competitors sold their cars.

When Dulian was transferred again Tucker went with the Ivor Schmidt agency, selling Stutz and other high-price jobs. He had no great difficulty in finding a market for these and made a reputation selling cars other salesmen could not move. Later he moved to the John T. Fisher Motor Company which handled Chrysler. In a very short time he became general sales manager. While selling Chryslers he made a connection with Pierce Arrow.

After two years in Memphis, Tucker was appointed regional manager for Pierce Arrow, working out of the factory in Buffalo, so once again he moved his family to Lincoln Park. He stayed with Pierce Arrow two years, leaving in 1933 to sell Dodges for Cass Motors in Detroit. He never liked to get far from the motor capital of the world.

While still in Memphis, Tucker started what was to become an annual pilgrimage for many years when he went to the Memorial Day race at Indianapolis. There he first met Harry

A. Miller, one of the greatest engine designers in automotive history. It was one of Preston's fixed purposes to meet all the old and new pioneers in the automobile business, and Miller was one of the real top-notchers among them. They became close friends, and they made an ideal combination. Tucker, still dreaming of his car, knew a man like Miller could contribute to it, and he believed that Miller could help to design the kind of motor he wanted.

Tucker was by now a recognized leader in automobile promotion and sales. Miller was at the apex of a brilliant career building race cars that dominated the "500" where Miller engines won more races than any other ever entered. Tucker didn't merely admire the Miller engine; he felt that an adaptation of that engine was what he wanted in his stock car.

The eccentric Miller would have commanded respect in any machine shop in the world. Of medium height, quiet and soft spoken, his sharp, pointed mustache was part of his pride and personality. His quiet way of giving orders contrasted sharply with the more volatile Tucker. One of Miller's chief aversions, Tucker said, was adjustable wrenches, and whenever he found a man using one he would take it away from him and bring him a set of end wrenches, of which he seemed to have an inexhaustible supply. He would tell the man: "Use a wrench that fits! If you haven't got one then *get one.*" If he found the man afterwards using an adjustable wrench again he might fire him, if he happened to be in a bad mood. Miller knew exactly what he wanted and how to get it, and these were qualities also possessed by Tucker. They were friends until Miller's death in 1943 from cancer, when he was sixty-eight years old.

Miller was credited with introducing aluminum bodies for racing cars, front drive and four-wheel-drive racers, and four-alloy pistons, superchargers, downdraft carburetors and four-wheel hydraulic disc brakes. Six racing cars he built for the Gulf Oil Company had rear engines with four-wheel drive. While Miller was working on the Gulf job, Tucker met Edward (Eddie) Offutt, who was considered one of the best engineers in the business by the racing fraternity at Indianapolis. Offutt later went with Tucker in Chicago, and was chiefly responsible for the final Tucker engine.

Miller's first complete race car was entered in the Vanderbilt Cup race in 1906, and Miller Specials are still racing today. The original Miller engine was taken over by Fred Offenhauser, who sold out to Meyer-Drake. (The Meyer in "Meyer-Drake" was Louis Meyer, only three-time winner of the "500" except Wilbur Shaw and Mauri Rose, coming in first in 1928, 1933 and 1936.) Offutt worked with Meyer-Drake on the Offenhauser engine, a direct descendant of the original Miller engine and still top dog on the tracks.

"Harry and Preston were just alike in a lot of ways," Mrs. Tucker recalled, "and it was simply maddening. One day we were driving to Indianapolis from Pittsburgh to see the race and the radio in the car wasn't working right.

"They stopped by a gas station in some little town in Ohio and Edna—Mrs. Miller—and I had to sit there drinking pop half the afternoon while they took that radio all apart. There wasn't one place to get anything to eat and all we could do was sit. They had parts spread all over the fenders and the hood, but when they finally got it back together it worked."

Miller and Tucker, Inc., was formed in 1935 to build racing cars and marine engines, and their first job was building ten cars for Henry Ford, with souped-up V-8 engines. They set up a plant on West Lafayette Street in Detroit where Offutt was a frequent visitor. Many of Tucker's ideas for his own automobile came from his association with Miller, which continued after the Ford contract was finished some months later and Tucker moved to Indianapolis. Miller set up a place there where Tucker often stopped in to talk shop, and they worked together on various projects until Miller's death.

After the Ford contract was finished Dick Cott, who owned the Dodge dealership in Detroit where Tucker had worked, opened the Packard Indianapolis agency on Meridian Street. Tucker went there as general manager, later becoming a partner. He finally was living in Indianapolis, his Mecca for years, and the Packard agency developed into a big operation. Tucker began to live in a style that matched his position.

First they rented a big house in Williams Creek, an exclusive suburb, with a series of decorative pools which the younger of the five children used for swimming, and a gymnasium complete with a basketball court. But the rarefied atmosphere was too stuffy for Tucker, who bought a small farm near Noblesville, about twenty miles away.

While selling Packards, Tucker, as usual, would trade for anything. He would take in jewelry, watches, furs, dogs, horses—anything which he could later sell to make a profit.

One day a bus pulled into the yard and out came a German with twenty-six dogs and put on a show for the kids. Tucker had just sold the German a Packard touring car, taking in the bus and twenty-six Dalmatians and English setters, a dog act the German had been working with circuses. After the show they drove the bus back to the garage to sell and took the dogs to the farm, where Tucker hired a man to take care of them until they got possession of the farm two weeks later. When they moved in there were still more dogs, which the German had told them they could expect almost any day now.

Around the house was a wire fence with a top rail of two-by-fours, and any time of the day they could see a line of dogs walking along the top of the fence. The children set up a wagonwheel tire, and the dogs kept jumping back and forth through it. When Mrs. Tucker opened the back door to shake out a dust mop, dogs would start jumping over the handle.

"One weekend when we were gone I guess the setters found out they were bird dogs," Mrs. Tucker said. "When we got back there were only twenty chickens left in a flock of fifty-seven blooded White Rocks that came with the farm. I told Preston he had to start getting rid of all those dogs."

Some they sold, others they gave away until they were down to a few Dalmatians. Then Tucker took in a five-gaited horse on a trade and the children rode all over the countryside until the horse was entered in a show. Tied in an improvised stall, Rex kicked the hell out of a prize horse in the next stall, and was finally sold to somebody who had more time to take care of him.

"Preston really felt bad about selling Rex," Mrs. Tucker said. "When he went to the pasture that horse would gallop clear across the field and take a handkerchief out of his pocket. He followed Preston around like a big dog."

The magnetic quality of Tucker attracted animals as well

as men. He had the knack of making friends because he accepted people at their face value and instilled confidence in others. It was instinctive with him—and it earned him a host of friends among the Midwest farmers and auto workers who recognized him as one of their own. Paradoxically, this same open, expansive quality was to make enemies for him when he moved in the world of high finance—a world in which cunning and reserve and polish were highly prized and where he was regarded as something of an interloper.

5

Into the Big Time

WHILE HE WAS IN AN INDIANAPOLIS HOSPITAL IN 1937, RE-
covering from an appendicitis operation, Tucker got the idea
of making a high-speed combat car. Newspapers were filled
with rumors of war and Tucker was reading Tolstoy's "War
and Peace." He believed war was on the way, and now was
the time to go ahead with his idea.

So after three lush years in Indianapolis he moved to Ypsilanti—about thirty miles west of Detroit—and bought a big
house on a double lot. At the back of the lot was a large barn
which he remodeled into a two-story building, adding sections as the new operation expanded. He set up a machine
shop on the first floor, offices along one side and put engineering and drafting rooms on the second floor.

Behind the building next to the alley were dynamometers
for testing engines. The bases are still there, along with 440-
volt electric lines and four-inch water mains. He called his
new operation, which was formed in 1940, the Tucker Aviation Corporation. This was the first Tucker corporation.

The combat car was spectacular, reaching a speed of 117

miles an hour, and it mounted a power-operated gun turret designed by Tucker and his engineers. Army officials said they didn't have any use for that kind of speed, but they were tremendously impressed by the gun turret. Mrs. Tucker still has a small model which he took with him on trips to Washington for conferences with government officials.

"Preston always carried that model in a pillow case," Mrs. Tucker said, "and when I went along I took a supply of clean ones. None of our children ever got the attention that Preston gave that precious model of his."

His persistence paid off and he got contracts for building the turrets. When operations outgrew the shop in Ypsilanti they took over one of the Graham-Paige plants on Warren Avenue in Detroit, and when that still couldn't handle the business, the job was sub-contracted to other companies. But here Tucker's luck failed him for the first time. The war started and the government confiscated his patents and royalty rights. Years later he was still suing other companies for royalties on turrets they had manufactured under his patents.

One of the engineers working for him at Ypsilanti was Jimmy Sakuyama. A graduate of Iowa and Wisconsin universities, Jimmy had worked with Miller and Fred Deusenberg and with the Chevrolet brothers. Tucker said that in 1929 he designed a four-in-line air-cooled light plane engine that passed government tests the first time it was run. Tucker met Sakuyama at Indianapolis.

Jimmy could have been the original prototype for the traditional Japanese of comedy. Short, with coarse black hair, he wore glasses with thick lenses, and his voice was a disconcertingly loud, monotonous singsong. When he talked he smiled, whether there was anything to smile about or not, and his bland expression gave not the slightest hint of what he might be thinking about. A sort of "Mr. Moto" at the drafting board, he was a genius in his way and Tucker recognized it.

When the war started and they began rounding up enemy aliens, Jimmy became desperate. He said he came from a noble family in Japan, that he had disgraced his family and he would never go back. He said he would kill himself first. Tucker told him not to worry, went to Washington, and had Jimmy paroled to him. So Jimmy lived in a trailer behind the plant, where he raised some chickens and one duck, which went under the trailer to sleep at night.

While he was a good engineer and an expert draftsman, Jimmy's weakness was the bottle, and he went on periodic bouts that usually ended in the hospital. It finally developed into a routine. Jimmy could tell when he had reached the hospital stage. He would dress over his pajamas, go to the hospital and lie down and wait for a doctor to come and check him over.

The hospital found him something of a problem, because as soon as he began to feel better he would dress and go downtown and buy boxes of candy, come back and go to bed and give the candy to the nurses. One day he went back to his trailer and killed and dressed a chicken, which he brought back to the hospital, asking the nurse to have it fixed for his dinner.

At the shop they were working two shifts part of the time, and sometimes they worked all night. Most of the technicians lived in Tucker's big house, where Mrs. Tucker had her table full three times a day. She said there was one time when the big stator ring on which the turret turned had to be ready the next day, and all the men were too tired to work on it.

"Preston told them to go to bed, that he would do it himself. The men didn't think he could. Right after dinner he and I went out to the shop and he started the lathe. It was a special setup and he had me turning it on and off while he checked it with a micrometer.

"I was getting nervous because we had a lot of money tied up in that ring and we couldn't afford to buy another one. It was some kind of special alloy and we had to wait a long time for delivery. So I kept telling him, 'Be careful, you're taking off too much.'

"Finally he got disgusted and told me to go in and go to bed. He worked out there by himself all night, and by morning he had it finished."

The men may have been surprised but Tucker wasn't, because the setup was his idea in the first place. The first job was only a development contract so they couldn't afford special equipment, but Tucker improvised a weird combination of an old belt-driven lathe and a horizontal milling machine.

Mrs. Tucker believes at least a million dollars worth of

engineering was done in that barn, and there are still Detex watch clock stations on the outside of the house and the barn, where a watchman checked in every hour.

During one of his trips to Washington, Tucker met Andrew J. Higgins, the New Orleans ship tycoon who was building torpedo boats and had contracts for 200 of the famous Liberty ships, using the same assembly line methods Kaiser was using on the West Coast.

Higgins and Tucker decided they had a lot of common interests, and in a meeting later in New Orleans they made a deal. The conference started at 6 o'clock in the afternoon, and Tucker said ten minutes later they wrote and signed a contract in longhand, which was made official after the lawyers worked it over. The deal was announced by Higgins on March 21, 1942.

It wasn't in the book that two men as highly individual as Higgins and Tucker could get along, but the deal looked like a natural at the start. Higgins, short with red hair and blue eyes, was like a little dictator, whom many believed would be the Henry Kaiser of the South. Slightly paunchy, he was an impressive bon vivant in white suits and panama hats and fitted perfectly into life in New Orleans, for he loved fine food and was a lavish entertainer. Tucker people said he was overbearing, and he was happiest with a lot of big projects all going at once. In his small world Higgins was a big operator and, like Tucker, a colorful personality who was always good for headlines.

Under their agreement Tucker became a vice president of Higgins Industries and would set up a separate plant for the new Higgins-Tucker Aviation division to mass produce gun turrets and engines for Higgins' boats.

Tucker's turrets were mounted on some of Higgins' fast torpedo boats, and spectacular demonstrations were staged on Lake Ponchartrain for the U.S. Navy, Marine Corps officials and representatives of the British Navy. Using balloons for targets, the boats sped around the lake shooting them down like clay pigeons.

Tucker took all his people from Ypsilanti and Detroit, about seventy families, and started operations in a plant on Scott Street in New Orleans. Jimmy was there in his trailer, across from the plant in a parking lot. Also there was Art Chevrolet, who went with Tucker after the racing team broke up. A frequent visitor was Eugene (Gene) W. Haustein, former race driver who was working with an armament company. Haustein, who later went with Tucker in Chicago as test driver and all-around trouble shooter, drove in four Speedway races, finishing fifth in 1935 in a Miller Special, the same car Louis Meyer won with in 1933. Tucker moved his family, which now included five children, into a big old house on Gentilly Boulevard.

"Preston worked the hardest I've ever seen a man work," said his wife. "He was nervous, and he got so thin he walked as if he were crippled. The doctor finally told him to get clear away from the plant on weekends and take it easy. We used to leave early Friday afternoon and go to the Edgewater Hotel in Gulfport. Preston would lie around and sleep most of the time, and we'd go back Sunday night."

One Sunday night they got back late and the whole crowd was in shorts, swimming suits and barefooted. When they started into the house they saw a big barrel. Tucker's youngest daughter, Marilyn, then fifteen, took off the lid and screamed. It was full of crabs.

The watchman said they were a present from Higgins, and when nobody knew what to do he explained how to cook them. It was too late to buy anything, but they picked some bay leaves in the back yard and found some lemons and peppers in the house. They got a big kettle and put it on the gas stove, lighting all three burners.

About this time the barrel tipped over and big crabs began squirming all over the floor. People jumped on the counter, climbed on tables and chairs while the crabs took over. Someone went to the garage and found some laths which they broke in two and used like chopsticks, picking up the crabs and dropping them into the kettle. All the time Marilyn was standing on a chair screaming:

"No, not *alive!*"

It took the rest of the night to get them all cooked, but they had crabs for breakfast and said they were terrific.

Tucker and Higgins worked together about a year, building and testing various boats and landing craft. But they were too much alike to get along. Both were impatient of detail, and both were lavish with money. Higgins was fighting with the government over some canceled contracts, and Tucker was fighting with Higgins. The deal finally blew up and Tucker went back to Ypsilanti. Higgins sued for $118,000 but the suit was dropped.

In Ypsilanti, Tucker rented a large metal building about a block from the house, set up a machine shop and went back to producing war materials, and the watchman had one more station to check on his rounds. In every spare moment Tucker was now working on plans for a new automobile. He thought the end of the war would be an ideal time to bring out a completely new car, because the entire industry, in the beginning at least, would be stuck with pre-war models.

Jimmy started working on the big opposed engine Tucker wanted, and Tucker took suspensions and other parts from racing cars to study, and determine how to adapt them for a fast, powerful passenger car. He hired an artist, Josephine Chatham, to sketch up his ideas, and her illustrations were used in the *Pic* story.

A new man joined the staff at Ypsilanti—Dan Leabu, an engineering graduate from the University of Michigan who had worked twelve years with Ford in tool design and electrical experimental projects. Later in Chicago he was active in final design of the Tucker automobile. Leabu at first sight wasn't a man who stood out. He wasn't talkative and hesitated to offer suggestions, in conferences or even conversations. Rather like a big bear, he was never obtrusive, but when some crisis came up and something needed to be done fast, it would very likely be Leabu who did it. He could operate any machine in the shop but, more important, he could handle the men who were hired to operate them, whether there were four or four hundred. Completely loyal to Tucker, he would take on any assignment without the least hesitation, from getting some part made fast to meeting with some millionaire on financing when Tucker was tied up. Leabu was more than an employee or associate of Tucker— he was also a friend.

By 1944 the business was going strong, but the end of the war was in sight and the shop was filled with orders that might be canceled any time. Tucker already had formed a loose organization to help promote his new automobile, and was negotiating with several companies to get it built.

It was at this stage that I went to Ypsilanti, met Tucker for the first time, and later wrote the story that got his venture off the ground. This was in December of 1945, and Tucker immediately started recruiting experienced automobile men to strengthen his small group. Many he had known intimately for years, and others became interested after the story of his new automobile made the newspapers and magazines.

Earlier, while talking with people in Chicago, trying to get a deal put together, Tucker had met Abraham (Abe) Karatz, who said he believed he could find a broker who would handle a stock issue. Karatz also said he understood Chrysler's Chicago Dodge plant was to be declared surplus, and that it would be ideal for building automobiles.

In Ypsilanti I first met Karatz, and I was immediately impressed with his intensity, his supreme confidence and his tremendous knowledge of people and places. Heavy but not fat, he had a quick smile and a deep penetrating voice that seemed to override doubts and problems by sheer volume. In time, after we became friends and he was "Abe," I learned his most serious weakness: his ambitions were always far ahead of his capabilities, and his thinking could have affected the entire Tucker operation. Always he was shooting for the one big deal that would run into millions, and I have repeatedly seen him pass up small deals in which he could pick up a few thousand because he wanted to pyramid them into a multi-million dollar promotion. In Tucker, he saw a man who could front the deals he could only dream about.

Next to promotions, which were Abe's life, he loved to eat, and he seemed to be equipped with some kind of radar to find the finest eating places in any city. It was occasionally embarrassing. If he happened to be low on money at the time he might borrow twenty dollars or so, and then he would take you out to dinner and insist that you eat more, maybe at five dollars a plate, on your own money. Yet as far as I know he was completely honest, and in his work for Tucker and the corporation he was tireless, with endless patience, and completely loyal.

There was one flaw in Karatz' record, which to us seemed small and unimportant: he had served time in Joliet for what the state charged was some kind of insurance fraud. He made no secret of it and Tucker considered it unimportant, though later Tucker's enemies seized on it as a weapon against him, charging that Tucker was a crook from the start because he was associated with Karatz.

Tucker meanwhile had developed into an impromptu public speaker who ranked with the best. He had none of the tricks of professional orators yet he was convincing, seemingly because his personality came through in spite of his ineptness with language. In his use of common words, and his frequent errors in grammar, he was sometimes compared with the late Huey Long, who won the solid support of the Louisiana bayou parishes with his backwoods mannerisms. Yet there was a difference: observers said Long cultivated his mannerisms for effect, but Tucker's were natural. It was Tucker himself talking, using the only language he knew.

So far, Tucker's speaking had been confined to small groups in his home, or office or hotel suite. But soon his audiences would be larger, because the deal was almost ready to roll. He was now ready for big deals and he saw himself as the center of the whole operation. He was beginning to taste power and enjoy it, realizing it was the only path to a success he was determined to achieve.

_____ *Part Two*

While the World Waited

_____ **6**

Growing Pains

WITH TUCKER'S LONG AND VARIED EXPERIENCE IN THE AU-
tomotive field and his proven sales record, his initial announcement of an entirely new automobile aroused the
immediate interest of many veterans in the industry. While
many believed some of Tucker's ideas were visionary or impractical, they saw enough features that could be used to make
the idea of a new company entirely feasible.

The first organizational meeting was held in the Detroit
Athletic Club and ended with an "oust Tucker" movement
before there was even a corporation. The main trouble with
this meeting seemed to be that early promoters in the deal
wanted too big a slice for their efforts, failing to realize that
a lot of high-power promotion would still have to be done to
get it off the ground. It finally ended in a squabble over per-
centages and Tucker walked out. It was about the only time
I ever saw Tucker act out of character. He stood up, said
"Good day, gentlemen," and walked out the door. He must
have read the phrase in a book, or maybe heard it in a movie.

It was the end of the first scene in the Tucker drama, and

probably the deciding factor in moving operations to Chicago a short time later. Tucker knew that the enmity of recent associates in Detroit, with their close ties in the industry, could be fatal if he tried to fight them on their own ground. When he finally moved the entire operation to Chicago, the only experienced automotive men still with him were Robert Pierce, Fred Rockelman and Ray Rausch. It was then that he formed the Tucker Corporation to make automobiles in 1946.

Pierce was a peppery little Scot with red hair, who came over from England in 1921 and, after working some years with Price, Waterhouse & Company, certified public accountants in Detroit, became controller of Briggs Manufacturing Company, world's largest independent body manufacturers. Pierce was secretary-treasurer and a director when he left Briggs, and he didn't go with Tucker because he needed money. Pierce saw something in Tucker's plans that appealed to his lively but practical imagination—a chance to do something big and important in the automotive field, and to have the fun of lighting a time bomb under the conservative skeptics in Detroit, who already were deriding Tucker as a screwball whose whole idea was a joke.

Pierce helped break up that first meeting when he pulled out a checkbook and suggested that everybody ante $5,000 to get things started. Some of the people who were yelling the loudest about percentages couldn't match the $5,000.

Rockelman had a long and distinguished career with the Ford Motor Company, was vice president of the Ford-owned Detroit, Toledo and Ironton Railroad, and later sales manager for the entire Ford organization. Portly and impressive in appearance, he had an open German face that radiated honesty, and a cultivated informality which put newcomers immediately at ease. He was a big man who, easily and informally, called important visitors by their first names shortly after they were introduced. And he was unquestionably a big man in the industry and around Detroit. He left Ford in 1930 to become president of Chrysler's Plymouth division, and during the war headed the Detroit office of Douglas Aircraft Company.

Rockelman later brought in Cliff Knoble as director of advertising, and Knoble came with Tucker after serving many years as advertising manager for Chrysler and later as account executive for Ruthrauff and Ryan, national advertising agency.

Ray Rausch was a director at Ford and later supervised manufacturing in all Ford divisions except the Willow Run plant. Shortly before the war ended, when all the companies held press conferences telling their plans for postwar production, Rausch easily stole the show for Ford with his calm announcement of what Ford would have and when. Spokesmen for most of the other companies hedged or answered questions with double talk, apparently lacking the authority or confidence that Rausch had.

Shortly after the first organization meeting Tucker moved his headquarters to the Blackstone Hotel in Chicago, the one city outside Detroit which he believed was ideally located for manufacturing automobiles. Chicago had long wanted an automobile plant and several previous attempts had failed. Except for highly specialized manufacturing, Chicago in many ways was a better location than Detroit, with a strong machine tool industry, steel mills and foundries and a good labor pool left over from war production.

Transportation facilities were equally advantageous. Chicago was a major railroad center, had one of the busiest air terminals in the world, water transportation that even included seagoing vessels, and the Illinois Waterway which reached from Chicago to New Orleans and the Gulf.

Tucker already had a covetous eye on the huge Dodge plant in Cicero, not far from the municipal airport, which during the war built B-29 engines and was then the biggest white elephant on the hands of War Assets Administration. The WAA was pledged to lease or sell the plant wherever it would be of greatest public value. Covering 475 acres, the plant boasted a main building that was the largest in the world under one roof, and separate buildings included a power plant and foundries for iron, aluminum and magnesium.

During the early part of 1946 Tucker concentrated on building up his staff and trying to negotiate some kind of a deal to get the Dodge plant.

Rockelman became vice president and director of sales, and did a magnificent job of organizing the sales department. Pierce was a vice president and treasurer, later resigning but continuing to serve as consultant to Tucker. Pierce didn't need the money and didn't want the responsibilities of the job. Rausch started as vice president in charge of manufacturing, but resigned before arrangements were completed for the stock issue.

When, in an early brochure, Tucker presented his executive staff under the heading "From the Top Ranks of Industry," he wasn't exaggerating. In addition to Pierce and Rockelman there was Hanson Ames Brown, vice president, who had been with Studebaker and Chrysler, had been assistant comptroller for General Motors in Detroit and was later vice president and director of all GM Canadian divisions. Ben G. Parsons, vice president in charge of engineering, was president and owner of the Fuelcharger Corporation in Detroit, specializing in fuel injection systems for aircraft and automobiles. Others were equally impressive, and for director of sales Tucker brought in Dulian, who had given him his first full-time job selling cars.

Another old friend who joined him in the new venture was Max Garavito, a Columbian who had his own export-import business in New York. Tucker first met him in the early 30s during one of his many trips to New York, and their acquaintance developed into a lifelong friendship. At the time Garavito was a lieutenant in the Columbian Air Force, during the war between Columbia and Peru, and was stationed in New York as an inspector of aircraft and armament purchases. Shortly after the sales department was started, Garavito organized the Tucker Export Corporation, using his own sales force and offices in New York.

During this period it became increasingly obvious that some kind of literature was needed beyond mimeographed handouts and the one brochure that had carried the operation this far, and which was already obsolete in view of design changes that had been agreed upon. In Washington one night a cab driver who didn't recognize Tucker talked all the way from the airport about the Tucker car, raising questions that Tucker would have spent all night answering if he had identified himself.

Contrary to popular belief, a brochure is not prima-facie evidence of intent to swindle somebody. When any kind of business reaches a certain stage there arises a multitude of questions that have to be answered, and a brochure, or pamphlet or folder of some kind, is the only practical solution. Without one, time must be wasted writing long repetitious letters of explanation. With any kind of adequate literature, it is only necessary to hand one brochure to a customer or enclose it with a letter.

Tucker had already commissioned a designer in Detroit to do an eighth scale clay model of the car, but the designer was making no visible progress in spite of repeated calls at his studio, and continued letters, telegrams and telephone calls. An eighth scale model is small, and if a designer knows what he is doing and works at it, he should be able to finish the job in two weeks. But this went on for months, and Tucker said he learned later that the man was only working occasional evenings and weekends.

One night the designer called Tucker in Chicago and said photographs of the model were in the mail and should arrive any minute.

"You will gasp!" he said excitedly.

Everybody was assembled waiting for the pictures and when they finally came, special delivery, everybody gasped. A few, including Tucker, almost turned green.

The photographs, made showing the model against natural backgrounds, weren't too bad, but the design itself was sad. Above the doors it was somewhat similar to the Mercedes 300 SL, with window glass curving in at the top. But the radius of the curve made the top and windows together almost a half circle, so that a full-grown man couldn't have sat anywhere in either seat except square in the middle.

But this model was all that was available until the project could be started all over again, and Tucker was stuck with it. And he needed the brochure. There wasn't time to wait for another model, considering that another designer might take just as long and come up with nothing better.

If there had been money enough to turn the whole job over to a good agency—copy, layout and artwork—it would have been no great problem. But this was strictly a budget job. So three of us—E. D. Hill, a New York advertising man then working with Tucker, James E. Tripp, Chicago publicity man, and I—got a room in the Palmer House and turned out the complete copy and layout in a little over two days. A Chicago artist made some fast sketches and it was ready for the printer.

59

Nobody will ever know how Tucker kept scraping up money for constantly increasing expenses, but he did. During most of 1946 and the early part of 1947, Tucker's Ypsilanti company furnished most of the money to keep the deal rolling until funds were available from sale of franchises. Dan Leabu, who had started with Tucker as an inspector, was then plant manager at Ypsilanti, and he said their entire profits were sent to Chicago.

"We must have made more than $100,000 in less than two years, and we sent them every dollar we could spare," Leabu said.

As the months went by it became more and more evident to Tucker that he couldn't get private financing without sacrificing control, which meant his only alternative was a stock issue. Without exception, the men or groups able to underwrite the deal demanded complete control; and Tucker, at this stage, wasn't ready to turn control over to a bunch of bankers.

But his luck held, as it had in the past when he needed particular men in his organization. He already had met Floyd D. Cerf, an investment banker on La Salle Street, who told him that he could handle a stock issue "as soon as you have a semblance of an automobile and a plant to build it in."

It looked like a tough assignment, but Tucker never had the least doubt that he would make it. If anybody questioned his ability he could point to the men around him, and to the tremendous public response before he even had a model of the car.

7

Two Long Shots

TUCKER WORKED STEADILY THROUGH THE EARLY MONTHS OF
1946, but as Memorial Day came closer he began to grow
restless. The reason was simple: there was nothing important
enough to keep him away from Indianapolis, where he hadn't
missed a race in years. Talking about it one day, he got the
idea that a win at the famous "500" would climax his buildup
for the two biggest hurdles ahead—getting the Dodge plant
and putting over a stock issue.

Most of his associates were against the idea on grounds
that the odds were too long, but since Tucker was paying for
it they didn't argue too much. George Barringer of Indianapolis, a contender in five Speedway battles, had one of the
six rear-engine racing cars that Harry Miller had built for the
Gulf Oil Corporation, so Tucker bought the car and hired
Barringer to drive it.

Entered as the "Tucker Torpedo Special," it had many of
the features Tucker planned for his passenger car, including
an aluminum head and block cast in a single unit, individual
wheel suspension and hydraulic disc brakes. The engine was

a straight six with a supercharger, and was the only one entered that used ordinary gasoline. It had 275 horsepower and had been clocked at 180 miles an hour in trial runs on the salt flats at Bonneville, Utah.

Many companies enter "Specials" for the publicity of just having been in the race, and none of the "Specials" ever made any pretense of being a stock car. Any stock automobile ever built would be lucky to even qualify, and nothing short of a miracle could carry one through the whole grind.

"We aren't greatly concerned whether we win or lose the race," Tucker told reporters, which wasn't strictly the truth. "Many things can happen before and during the race, and the best car may not always win."

Tucker was playing a long shot and counting on the car to at least make a good showing. Barringer qualified easily and drove the Special at a terrific pace for twenty-six laps, when he was forced out by gear trouble. It was too tough a job to tackle in a pit stop, so for him the race was over.

For Tucker, the failure of his Special even to finish was disappointing, but not a total loss because he had his own entry for the first time and a personal stake in the hurry and excitement around him. Many of the immortals of racing were there—Ray Harroun, Ralph De Palma, Barney Oldfield, Ab Jenkins and Louis Meyer. Ralph Hepburn set an all-time qualifying speed of 133.944 mph driving a Novi Governor Special, front-wheel drive with a 500-horsepower supercharged Winfield engine. He too was forced out of the race, with engine trouble.

Tucker was popular around the Speedway and when his entry lost, the press gave him a break, either ignoring the car's failure or mentioning that it was forced out of the race without adding any great detail. Among the reporters was John Jenkins, automotive writer for the *Chicago Daily News*, who later joined Tucker as public relations director for the advertising agency which handled the account.

With the race over Tucker went back to work, and before long he topped his first hurdle—getting the plant.

In setting his sights on the Dodge plant, Tucker was playing even longer odds than the race, and with considerably more at stake. Built at a cost of more than $170,000,000, it was completely modern, with offices, conference rooms, cafeteria, hospital quarters, and parking space for thousands of automobiles. Against him were other bidders with more money to invest, but in his favor were provisions of the Surplus Property Act, and the least important of its provisions was financial return to the government. The objectives in disposing of such plants were sound: to get them into operation and put people to work.

Tucker had been negotiating with War Assets since January after the plant was advertised for sale, and the prestige of his associates was an important factor in finally getting it. Most of his contact with War Assets was with Oscar H. Beasley, special assistant to the administrator.

"Tucker called me one day from Chicago," said Beasley, "and outlined a proposal, saying he would be in Washington the next day to see me. When he came in I asked him how much actual money he had and he said $12,000. Where? In the bank at Ypsilanti. While he sat there in my office I phoned his bank and asked them a lot of questions. They told me that Tucker was the son of a family that had been in the machine tool business there and that he had an honorable reputation. As to his capacity to operate such a plant they weren't prepared to say. They told me the $12,000 was there as he said."

When Beasley went to the Reconstruction Finance Corporation to check Tucker's credit further, he received a wire from RFC Acting Assistant Manager R. H. Garfield saying:

"Pursuant to Mr. Preston Tucker's request, you are advised that RFC has made two loans to Ypsilanti Machine Tool Company. Payments on the loans were always made definitely on time. In fact the loans were paid in full prior to their maturity."

"I told Tucker I wouldn't recommend that his offer be accepted for that amount as an initial payment," Beasley continued, "but I added several million dollars to the figure and told him if he could put things on a sound financial basis there might be some possibility we could go along with him. He raised his cash figure to $25,000 and his proposal was sent to the Board of Review. I thought the thing was dead then, and had no more to do with it for several weeks."

Tucker submitted his proposal with a check for $25,000 and about the first of July received a "letter of intent," accepting the bid and setting up a schedule for future payments of $150,000 a month beginning in August. Handling of that $25,000 check was later denounced by Homer Ferguson, Republican Senator from Michigan, who charged that it was never cashed. Beasley said as far as he knew, the check simply got lost.

"As far as I know it was an entirely honest deal, and if Tucker benefited by the check being lost for a while he was simply fortunate, because I don't believe there was anything deliberate on anybody's part. Something like this happening wouldn't have been at all unusual, with the amount of work they had in the financial section at that time."

After it was apparent that months would be needed for War Assets to complete its inventory of the plant, a new lease agreement was reached canceling the monthly payments, and contingent on Tucker's having at least $15,000,000 capital by March 1 of the following year. Up to that time Tucker could use such space as was available to build pilot models and mockups.

The lease was to be for ten years beginning March 1 and called for a yearly minimum payment of $500,000 for the first two years, and $2,400,000 a year thereafter or three per cent of gross sales, whichever was the greater. The new lease included provisions for buying the plant and machinery.

While Tucker's negotiations with War Assets were largely through Beasley and the Board of Review, he worked every angle he could find to shorten the odds. No stranger to Washington, he knew the angles and enlisted representatives and senators, politicians in both parties, union leaders, financial men in New York and Chicago, influential people in government—anybody he could reach who showed any promise at all of being able to help.

Almost everybody who was working with Tucker at the time, and who got within guided missile range of Washington, claimed most or all of the credit for getting the plant. Some of them, of course, played a bigger part than others, but it is unlikely that any one person or factor was responsible. Tucker's own determination and persistence convinced War Assets that he could take over the Dodge plant and create employment.

One of the most influential men who wanted him to get the

plant was Walter P. Reuther, president of the CIO United Auto Workers. Reuther wired War Assets:

"We are extremely desirous that this plant be used as a complete productive unit for the manufacture of automobiles. We believe such use will provide maximum amount of employment and provide for maximum utilization of productive capacity both for the best interest of the workers involved and the nation. Our understanding is that Preston Tucker's proposal is the only one which appears to meet these objectives."

Copies were sent to President Truman, John R. Steelman, then head of the reconversion program, and other government officials and senators.

Whoever was responsible, Tucker had the plant. Tucker Corporation had already been formed, and he announced in the middle of July that they would set up temporary offices at the plant while WAA started inventory of $30,000,000 worth of machinery.

Offices were on the second floor of the main building, and rattling around the offices and the huge empty plant the first several weeks was like playing tag in the Rose Bowl. It would have taken a week just to look it over, riding a scooter.

Desks and chairs were pushed into position, folding tables were set up, telephones connected and people went to work. There wasn't even a receptionist yet but men and women lined up at the front entrance looking for work. Mail came by truckloads and telephone operators were swamped with calls from people who wanted jobs, some who wanted to be dealers and others who were just plain curious.

Less than seven months after Tucker announced his new automobile he was set up in the biggest manufacturing plant in the world, and all he had left to do was raise twenty or thirty million dollars and build an automobile. That did not faze Tucker in the least. He felt confident that he was on the road to big success.

8

Screwballs, Phonies
and Characters

IT WAS INEVITABLE THAT AN OPERATION WITH THE GLAMOUR and possibilities of the Tucker deal would attract a lot of characters, five percenters and opportunists who saw a chance for a fast buck.

It must have been some form of tropism. Screwballs and phonies had only to sniff the air, and then they would flutter their wings, check their gas and oil gauges and, with unerring instinct, head straight for Tucker. They came so fast there wasn't time to sort them out. For every legitimate operator who managed to reach Tucker there must have been twenty oddballs, each with connections or deals that would solve all his problems.

Here are a few of the oddballs who showed up:

There was J. Worthington Clump, a millionaire from Cleveland who had been introduced to Tucker as a potential "angel." J. Worthington Clump wasn't his name, of course, and the Cleveland millionaire was a bad investment for Tucker Corporation long before there were either stockholders or dealers. Headquarters at the time were in the Blackstone Hotel in Chicago, where Tucker was working around the clock trying to put a deal together which wouldn't require a stock issue.

Clump had a beard that partly covered a dirty white shirt, baggy clothes and holes in the soles of his shoes. But before he left Chicago he went to one of the big banks and cashed a check that proved he could dress like Gandhi if he felt like it. Among his various holdings, which included assorted public utilities and such, was the distillery that made Old Glockenspiel, which Clump said reverently was as fine a whiskey as ever caressed a man's tonsils.

"You don't just drink Old Glockenspiel," he said, with a faraway look in his eyes, like a man thinking of his mistress.

To savor Old Glockenspiel fully, it seemed, you sniffed its bouquet like a fine brandy, and rolled it around in your mouth to appreciate the sublime perfection of its gentle authority. Finally, you allowed a few drops to trickle sensuously down your throat.

With all this buildup, the next step obviously was to sample some Old Glockenspiel. The problem was how to get it, and nobody had the temerity to suggest they send down to the liquor store in the hotel.

So Clump got on the phone and called Cleveland. Night had fallen, so he must have routed some executive out of bed to explain that he must exert every effort to get some Old Glockenspiel to Tucker and his associates in the Blackstone Hotel. After a time whoever was at the other end called back—collect—and after a couple of more calls it was established that a certain liquor store in the Loop could supply this fine whiskey. He must have run up $40 or $50 in long distance calls, all on Tucker's bill. When the sample arrived it wasn't a case. It wasn't a fifth.

It was a pint.

Then there was Mustafa el-Hasim, who was in the rug business in Chicago and decided that a logical extension of his operation was Tucker distributorships in Iran, Cook County, Illinois, and a large portion of the Eastern Seaboard. El-Hasim reportedly had made his money in Iran during the war, building roads for the British who rewarded him handsomely with lend-lease money from the United States. The only way he could get it out of Iran in any sizable chunks was in the form of rugs, which he imported into the United States.

It was on a Friday, when Tucker had been in the plant only a few months, that someone connected with the United Nations in New York called Max Garavito, head of the Tucker Export Corporation in New York, to arrange a meeting with some friends who wanted to know more about Tucker. After dinner at the Waldorf they went to a Park Avenue apartment crammed with Persian rugs and Oriental furnishings, and arranged to fly to Chicago the following day.

"This fellow el-Hasim wasn't supposed to understand English," said Garavito, "but he understood everything. In the export business you learn a lot about people, and if you ever meet a man who's sharper than a Persian, he'll be another Persian. The whole weekend went so fast we didn't even have time to think. I never did know the name of that man from the United Nations. Everybody called him 'Your Excellency.'"

In Chicago they joined Tucker and some of his associates and were entertained lavishly in el-Hasim's home, where they met his brother, a professor who taught physics or something in one of the universities there. From there they went to the rug store on Wabash Avenue, under the elevated, where el-Hasim gave rugs to both Tucker and Garavito and wrote a check for $50,000 and signed three notes for $50,000 each.

Monday, Garavito and the people from New York went back on the Century, and when Garavito reached his office Tucker was calling to say el-Hasim had stopped payment on the check. Garavito and Tucker agreed there was no point arguing about it, and the best thing they could do was charge their time and expenses against the rugs and forget it, and be thankful they got off that easy.

Next morning, driving out to the plant, Tucker stopped at the rug store where el-Hasim didn't understand English again and sat to one side looking dumb, while his brother from the university carried the ball.

The professor explained it was all a big mistake.

"My brother, he not understand money," he said.

"For example, one day I say to him, 'I want to borrow twenty-five hundred dollars.' My brother say, 'Okay, you sign note.' I say, 'What, I sign note for lousy twenty-five hundred dollars? No! I not sign note!'

"My brother think is twenty-five *thousand* dollars. Ha ha! My brother not understand money."

"Ha ha," echoed el-Hasim, still looking like a poor immigrant who didn't understand the joke but wanted to be congenial.

So Tucker canceled the contracts and gave el-Hasim back his notes.

The wedding of Kevin O'Connell and a pretty little girl named Felice wasn't a major social event on the Tucker calendar, but it was an incident that added to the picture of an informal, friendly organization in which the president took a personal interest in the happiness and welfare of his employees. It made everybody who had a part in it feel good.

O'Connell worked in sales, where he had an excellent record and was considered one of the best men in the department. The wedding was held at the home of his immediate superior, Jack Grimes, who lived in Wheaton. According to O'Connell, it was love at first sight, and a whirlwind romance. Tucker and Grimes were both pleased that he was going to get married and settle down. They felt it would have a steadying effect.

The wedding ceremony was modest but impressive, and the bride—an attractive redhead—was completely charming with just the right degree of dewy happiness in her eyes. The groom was tall and handsome, with the traditionally distinguished look that goes with a touch of gray at the temples. Tucker gave the bride away, or maybe he was best man.

A slightly ribald touch was an impromptu duet on the front porch, just as the ceremony ended, when a couple of characters from the plant played "I Love You Truly" on a clarinet and baritone horn. When the minister left he hesitated briefly to give the pair a dirty look, and stamped out to his car. Maybe he didn't like music.

Some months later a magazine representative came through town and happened to mention that he knew O'Connell. Tucker told him about the wedding.

"What, again?" asked the man. "Hell, they've been mar-

69

ried twice before that I know of, once in Cincinnati and once in San Antonio.''

"Well, lots of people get divorced and then get married again," said Tucker.

"Yeah, sure," said the man, "but they didn't get divorced. They just got married again. It's a gimmick.''

The magazine rep explained that O'Connell, a former advertising man and something of a psychologist, had developed getting married into a special tool to be used for emergencies, when his job might have been getting shaky or he needed a new angle to strengthen an account. You don't ordinarily fire a man who just got married, is still starry-eyed and has a new bride to support.

Tucker didn't spread the story. O'Connell's succeeding marriages to the same wife seemed a bit unusual, but as far as anybody knew they weren't illegal, or even necessarily unethical. O'Connell was still one of the best men in the department, and as far as Tucker was concerned he didn't need the boost of a romance, whether it was a premiere or a re-run. If he hadn't been good, his getting married wouldn't have helped him much anyway.

O'Connell, unaware that his secret was out, kept on talking about his Chicago romance two years later. And some years later we found out that at least part of Felice's starry-eyed charm derived from the fact that she didn't have on her bifocals, and could just barely see where she was going.

Mr. Wu lived in Shanghai and he came through Chicago on the way to visit his daughter, who was studying to be a missionary in a school somewhere in Michigan. He wanted to see just two things in Chicago—the Tucker car and the girlie shows. With a healthy supply of yen stashed away in British banks in Hong Kong, he was interested in a distributorship for China, and he spent the day looking over the plant. The night he reserved for relaxation.

Planning a visual feast, an experienced guide starts with an appetizer and a salad, working up gradually to the main course. The tour started on West Madison Street, where Mr. Wu worked up an appetite in the lower- and middle-class strip joints. In one, where a statuesque lovely displayed particularly outstanding charms, Mr. Wu's guides were afraid for a moment that he was going to vault over the intervening tables and climb up on the stage. There was some speculation on what he would do if he made it.

Mr. Wu was 86 years old.

The last spot was the 606 Club on South Wabash. The star of the show was a supple siren who finished her act with whirling lights on the darkened stage, and the effect was something like a planetarium running in overdrive. Mr. Wu was fascinated.

Next morning, as we drove him to catch his train, traffic was heavy and it looked for a while as if he wouldn't make it.

"Do not worry," said Mr. Wu. "If I miss the train I go back to the 606 Club."

9

Seven-League Bootstraps

Lots of equipment was stored in the huge Dodge plant when Tucker and his associates moved in, including typewriters, mimeographs, adding machines and office furniture, but there still wasn't any money except what Tucker could scrape up by borrowing and making deals for his own block of "founder's stock," the value of which was still hypothetical.

But people staked out office space and went to work. There wasn't much engineering yet because space hadn't been cleared for working areas, and even if there had been there wasn't enough money to set it up. And this need for immediate money inspired the franchise program.

Selling franchises wasn't new. Tucker didn't invent it. But he was the first to make it a big operation with promise of raising enough money to get started. Altogether, thirty-three new companies were launched after the war to build automobiles.

Some of the new companies sold franchises, which may

have given Tucker the idea. Wherever he got it, Tucker was the only one in the organization who believed it would work. And he was the only one of all the newcomers who built up a franchise operation into the big money bracket, enough to make an actual start on design and production. Altogether approximately $6,000,000 was raised through sales of franchises.

Credit for success of the franchise program belongs largely to Fred Rockelman, whose background as sales manager for Ford gave him an immense and practical knowledge of the problems that had to be solved. Under his direction territories and quotas were set **up**, and the multitude of forms worked out to put the operation on a businesslike basis and—they hoped—offer prospective distributors and dealers a plan that was both fair and legal.

The first franchise plan, which was launched in July of 1946, set the price at $50 a car over a two-year period, with a provision to hold the money in escrow until enough was obtained to pay for preliminary design and start production. If the amount raised wasn't enough the money would be refunded. If enough was raised, initial $50 deposits would be credited to purchase of cars as they were delivered.

Interest in foreign countries had been tremendous since the car was first announced, so headquarters for this part of the franchise program were set up in New York. Max Garavito was the natural man to head it, since he was already well established in the export business and had contacts all over the world.

In September, when the franchise program had gotten off to a good start, the Securities & Exchange Commission moved in with what they called an "informal investigation," launching a series of probes that continued with hardly a break over the next three years. While there had been no stock issue yet, and theoretically at least SEC wasn't even involved, the Chicago SEC office said "franchise agreements then being entered into constituted a security within the meaning of the Act."

Although this was an unexpected snag that caught them at a critical time, Tucker and the sales department didn't argue, and made every effort to get along with SEC without discontinuing the program entirely. Lawyers for Tucker and SEC haggled for months, through conferences and interminable correspondence, trying to reach an agreement. Meanwhile the program lagged. It was hard to work up much enthusiasm when Tucker might have to give the money back and start all over.

Finally a new plan was worked out under which the buyer of a franchise didn't stand the ghost of a chance of ever getting his money back unless the company got into heavy production. While this may have scared some of the dealers out, it apparently was satisfactory to SEC, and months after the "informal investigation" was first announced Edward H. Cashion, SEC chief counsel, said:

"It is my opinion that the sale of these distributor and dealer franchises will not involve the sale of a security within the meaning of the Act."

In a letter outlining major features of the new plan, Rockelman wrote SEC:

"We believe that the dealer franchise agreement form is so drawn up that no individual purchasing such an agreement could be misled concerning the nature of the transaction. However, in order to further protect the corporation we will make it a practice of reviewing with each purchaser the nature of the transaction, and to satisfy ourselves that he is not purchasing the agreement under any misunderstanding or in reliance upon any facts which are untrue."

What this meant in simple English was that dealers who bought franchises were putting their money in a crap game, and that is exactly what many of them were told. Max Garavito, head of the Tucker Export Corporation in New York, told essentially the same story:

"Before we sign a franchise they have their lawyer in my office and I have my lawyer. I tell them if we do not build an automobile you don't get anything. You don't even get so much as one bolt. There is no misunderstanding. They understood very clear that the only way they can win is for us to win."

The new contract called for payment of $20 per car over a two-year period, with half of the amount in cash and the balance in notes, payable at the end of a twelve-month period. SEC approved the new arrangement as in no way constituting the sale of securities, its first objection, and got Tucker off the hook for immediate money when it spelled out the terms:

That "the monies received would not be refundable under any circumstances but would be used by the corporation forthwith for general corporate purposes."

While Tucker had high hopes for raising enough capital to get started through the franchise program, he realized he would need a lot of money after he finally got formal possession of the plant next March 1. With a firm lease already in his possession, contingent only on having $15,000,000 capital by that date, Tucker met with Cerf again and they signed an underwriting agreement on September 30. The first agreement was in longhand, and made official a few days later with a seventeen-page typed agreement signed by Tucker and Cerf. Two days later, on October 2, Cerf announced a $20,000,000 issue of common stock would be offered as soon as it could be cleared with SEC.

Up to signing of the underwriting agreement, meetings with Cerf had been mostly in his offices on La Salle Street, heart of Chicago's financial district. With the agreement signed, Cerf was seen frequently around the plant, and when he ventured an opinion he got attention. And with reason, because the future of the corporation was in his well-manicured hands, and his skill in setting up and handling the machinery to sell stock. Cerf had his own successful brokerage business long before he met Tucker, and his manner reflected his success. Short and balding, he rather resembled a miniature Buddha when he sat in one of his big office chairs with his legs crossed under him, in the belief that this improved his circulation. He was intense and single-minded, and we early learned not to make jokes about the stock issue or anything connected with it around him, because to Cerf there was nothing funny about money, least of all the even remote possibility of losing it.

With the underwriting agreement signed and the franchise program going strong again, Tucker was ready for the next step—developing a prototype automobile which, under his agreement with Cerf, was to be completed before the stock was sold.

Raising initial capital through sale of franchises was one of the boldest and most successful bootstrap operations in industrial history, but it could not be said that Tucker conned the dealers. They were in a king-size crap game, and most of them knew it.

10

The Battle
of Press Releases

BUT THE PROTOTYPE HAD TO WAIT, AND SO DID THE FRAN-
chise program and financing. A "Directive" hit Tucker square
below the belt before the new franchise plan was even well
under way, and arrangements for a stock offering had just
been completed. Enemies began to appear.

During the Roosevelt Administration there developed a system of government by decree, under which even minor officials practically made and enforced their own laws. In
practice, it was reversion to an almost feudal form of government, in which heads of departments and bureaus became
little dictators.

The instrument which accomplished this phenomenon was
called a "Directive," with which they could bypass standard
procedure, largely ignore law and frequently even bluff Congress. Such habits are heard to break, and even after the war
some officials were still solemnly issuing directives with all
the authority of tablets relayed by fast runners direct from
Mount Sinai.

When the smoke cleared away, the burning bush turned out

to be photographers' flashbulbs and the tablets just another directive. And instead of Moses, there was Wilson Wyatt, a politician who had once been mayor of Louisville and who for a time held a position of considerable power in Washington. Wyatt's title was Housing Expediter and he was head of the National Housing Agency.

Tucker by this time had moved his headquarters to the Drake Hotel and his associates were scattered over Chicago in hotels and apartments. Some were still commuting from their homes in Michigan, waiting to see if the deal was going to hold together before moving their families to Chicago. Tucker suspected that undercover work was going on against him. The first rumble came about two days before the Wyatt directive became headlines, when information came over the grapevine that "Somebody is trying to take the Dodge plant away from you."

Most of the Tucker crowd didn't take the threat seriously at first, thinking it was too fantastic, and one of his public relations advisers told him, "This is a political fight. You stay out of it." Tucker thought otherwise and he, Mrs. Tucker and I grabbed a train to Washington. By the time we got in, Tucker was in the headlines again and newsboys were shouting:

"Read all about it—Wyatt takes Tucker plant!"

On out-of-town newsstands we saw Chicago papers, and a crimson streamer of the *Herald American* dated October 28 said: TUCKER LOSES DODGE PLANT. It was the first hard blow.

In Chicago there were two immediate results: sale of franchises fell to a dribble and Cerf stopped lining up houses to handle the stock issue. There was no percentage buying franchises for a car that didn't even have a plant, and trying to sell the stock with the plant gone would be impossible.

In Washington the picture was even blacker. Wyatt insisted that War Assets cancel Tucker's lease and turn the plant over to the Lustron Corporation of Chicago to build prefabricated houses. (Lustron planned to make sheet steel sections coated with baked enamel for houses that would never need painting.) Wyatt also was backing Lustron for a loan of at least $12,000,000 from the Reconstruction Finance Corporation. When some of us inspected Lustron's first house later in Chicago, we wondered what would happen when a kid on a tricycle banged into one of those baked enamel panels.

Wyatt's directive said:

"The office of the Housing Expediter today issued a directive to the War Assets Administration ordering the allocation of the war-surplus Dodge-Chrysler plant at Chicago to the Lustron Corporation of that city. The directive was necessary because War Assets Administration had stated that it is bound by a prior commitment to the Tucker Corporation involving lease of this plant. The Tucker Corporation plans to produce a new automobile, if it can raise the necessary capital."

What burned Tucker up was the last line, "if it can raise the necessary capital," and he could have pointed out—though he thought it smarter not to—that to most people an automobile was more important than a house anyway.

He found an unexpected ally in George Allen, head of RFC and a confidant of President Truman, who flatly refused to even consider the loan to Lustron. When Wyatt rushed to the White House yelling "Foul!" Allen rushed right behind him, and when they came out together they issued a joint statement: "We are in complete disagreement." It was learned later that Wyatt had another directive, all ready to issue, which would have ordered RFC to loan Lustron $52,000,000.

Reporters late in 1946 laid siege to Tucker's suite in the Mayflower Hotel to follow one of the hottest stories that had hit Washington in weeks. War Assets stood by Tucker, saying as he did, that it was a firm lease and throwing the whole mess into the Attorney General's lap. Tucker threatened to sue the government for breach of contract, but he was bluffing and everybody knew it. If the government doesn't want to be sued about the only hope left is an Act of Congress. You've had it.

Overnight Tucker found himself right in the middle of a new battle in which the guns were mimeographs and the ammunition press releases. When one of the departments involved made a public statement Tucker had to be in there with his own press release, because he couldn't afford to wait and ad lib the answers when some lone reporter banged on the door at the hotel. Before it was over, five different government departments or agencies were involved, including the White House, all with their own publicity departments, and Tucker at one time or another was feuding with almost everybody except War Assets. And when they issued a statement, he had to back it up.

We felt like two against the world and it was fortunate that Vera had come along, because she provided a sympathetic sounding board while we planned strategy for the next day. A few weekends we got out of Washington, but it was hard to relax with more than a year's work going down the drain.

We found a small duplicating service that opened early in the morning and would cut stencils and run off releases while we waited, and this became headquarters for the Battle of Press Releases.

Sometimes a release couldn't be written before checking the morning papers to find out what had been said last, and I would dash them off while the man cutting stencils grabbed pages out of the typewriter before I even had a chance to make corrections. Frequently Tucker didn't know what he had said until he read the release in a cab on the way to another press conference. The various agencies and departments would have people planted in our press conferences, and one of us would sit in the back row at theirs, stealthily taking notes and trying to look like another visitor. But nobody was fooling anybody very much. Every agency had an edge of at least five to one on manpower, and between them they had enough press agents to snow us under.

We stayed in Washington a solid month, living largely on the cuff at the Mayflower, while the operation in Chicago slowed almost to a standstill. Many of the Tucker people in Chicago were ready to give up. Toward the last, when it began to look as if there were some chance of winning, a few showed up in Washington saying, "I knew you could do it. Stay in there and fight, boy!"

When War Assets refused to be impressed with the first directive, Wyatt, like De Lawd in "The Green Pastures," rared back and issued a new directive to give Lustron part of the plant. Next day Tucker told a press conference that the night before, at the urging of the Housing Agency, he had met with Carl G. Strandlund, president of Lustron, to discuss joint occupancy.

Tucker said he offered half a million feet in the main building or a million feet in other buildings, but Strandlund wouldn't settle for less than three million feet in the main building, which was most of it.

Wyatt's proposal was that they wait until March 1 to see if Tucker had the money he needed, and if he didn't Lustron would take over under the terms of his lease. Wyatt was wide open.

"If the need for pre-fabricated housing is so desperate," Tucker countered, "why is Mr. Wyatt still willing to wait until March 1 to get the Tucker plant—if he can get it then? In direct contradiction to his frenzied screams that housing must get under way immediately, Wyatt's office has already deferred progress more than three weeks trying to get this one particular plant."

Privately Tucker said, "The hell with him. If I lose the plant I'm dead. I'll either keep all of it or I'll lose it. If all they want is a fight, they've got it."

It was rapidly developing into a free-for-all. In Chicago the Building Commissioner said Lustron's houses couldn't be put up without changing the building code, and from the building trades came unofficial word that union members wouldn't touch pre-fabricated houses with a pole.

Wyatt enlisted the American Veterans of World War II, whose housing chairman blasted War Assets, charging that the agency "in the past has shown favoritism to speculators and war profiteers."

"It now proposes to betray the best hopes of veterans to get low-cost mass produced houses," said the Amvets' statement. In sheer bulk, the wordage was becoming impressive.

But the pace was beginning to slow down and Tucker feared that during the lull somebody might put over a fast one. What was needed, he decided, was a shot in the arm. What followed was the highlight of the whole episode, and it added two powerful enemies to his already formidable opposition.

First came a series of broadcasts by commentator and columnist Fulton Lewis Jr., who had a wide following across the nation, and who specialized in government stink stories. "That's the Top of the News as it Looks from Here," over the Mutual network, was accepted as gospel by an unofficial fan club that numbered thousands.

The story was right down Lewis' alley, all about backstage

81

intrigue in government, and Tucker added the element of suspense with a mysterious "Mr. X" who, he said, would be unmasked when the time was right. The first broadcast told of Tucker's gallant fight against the Housing Administration, and the demands of "Mr. X" for half a million dollars in stock and legal fees for services which, Tucker declared, were of no help whatever.

Then Drew Pearson joined the fray, identifying "Mr. X" as Theodore Granik, New York and Washington attorney and former counsel for the U. S. Housing Authority, which preceded NHA. Pearson predicted that an investigation would find Granik "blameless of wrongdoing."

Whereupon Republican Senator Homer Ferguson from Michigan charged in, opening an investigation before his Senate Surplus Property Committee. Witnesses included Tucker, Granik, Wyatt and officials from various agencies. Tucker said he had an agreement with Granik but it was solely for financing, and when Granik couldn't produce the deal was off.

Granik called Tucker's story "an unvarnished lie," and Wyatt swore there was no skulduggery in his office. The hearing ended up in pretty much of a draw, but it very probably started the enmity of Drew Pearson, whose broadcast next year knocked Tucker stock down from $5 to less than $3 overnight. In the hearing Granik was represented by Thurman Arnold, former trust buster in the Roosevelt Administration. Arnold's son was married to Drew Pearson's daughter, which may seem a tenuous relationship to start a war, but war it was from then on.

Certain of Fulton Lewis' colleagues would say that Tucker sold him a bill of goods in the "Mr. X" story, and that by the time Lewis woke up he was married to it and couldn't pull out without losing face. One former Tucker man said Lewis' leg man—I think it was Frank Morrison—still wouldn't talk to him four years later.

Granik later sued for more than a million dollars damages for breach of contract, claiming eight per cent of Tucker's stock and $180,000 legal fees, but the suit never came to trial. To what extent Tucker's charges were true only he and Granik knew, and they weren't likely to agree. But the "Mr. X" business served Tucker's purpose in keeping the story alive until somebody could be forced into taking action. If Tucker had quit anywhere along the line, Wyatt would have gobbled the plant.

These were blows at Tucker's prestige, below-the-belt punches which served to mar the popular conception of Tucker. A new and different myth was being created by his enemies, a conception of him that Tucker would have to correct, an idea he would have to fight with every ounce of energy and resource he could summon.

As when he was trying to get the plant, Tucker exerted every pressure he could to keep it. He was in constant touch with John R. Steelman, aide to President Truman. Late in October he received a letter from House leader John W. McCormack saying:

"Following my telegram to you, I am enclosing a copy of my telegram to Wilson Wyatt, which I am sending to you for your information." McCormack's wire to Wyatt said, "It would be a grave mistake to allow some other company under guise of making some kind of buildings to prevent Tucker company from going ahead with its plans."

One of Tucker's associates went to Reuther again, with the logical position that the Auto Workers would be out in the cold if the plant went to Lustron. And again, as when he got the plant, nearly everybody who took even a small part in the fight claimed credit for winning it. It could have been Reuther who saved the day, or it could have been a combination of people and influence.

One thing is sure: if Tucker hadn't jumped into the fight with both feet and stayed in it, he would have lost the plant, and been forced to make a new start with at least a year's work wasted.

After the excitement of the committee hearing died down, the Christmas holidays were close and it seemed unlikely that any action would take place until after New Years. So there was no point in staying around Washington.

Wyatt and his whole housing program were on the spot and nothing but the White House could save. He put it up to the President, who left on vacation without making a decision, leaving Wyatt the loser by a technical knockout. Early in January after Wyatt resigned, Frank Creedon, new Housing

Expediter, withdrew the Wyatt directive and Tucker was back in business.

But the fight had cost a lot of money and Tucker had lost a lot of time. More serious, he had lost much of his prestige, his organization had almost fallen apart and the franchise program would have to be started all over again.

The battle with Wyatt was over, but the war was just beginning. Tucker had gotten a glimpse of the kind of opposition he would have to overcome. It made him more resolute than ever. If there was to be a war, Tucker would be in there fighting. And the fight would require a tremendous load of work.

One of the first jobs was to create a body for the prototype which would live up to its advance billing.

_____ *11*

The Body Beautiful,
on Wheels

EARLY IN DECEMBER, DURING THE LULL IN THE HOUSING fight, I was complaining one day to one of the top men planning production that I wished to hell we had something better than the lousy art work we were using, because it was getting tougher to sell every day. It was too arty and stylized to start with and, worse still, even a layman could see that it was a long way from the six-passenger sedan Tucker said he was going to build.

The production man said he was just as disgusted as I was, and if he had even an idea as to what the body and chassis were going to look like he could at least start figuring out how to build it. That was what started the first actual work on final body design, and the entire job was completed in less than a month.

He built a big plywood board back in the main building, eight feet high and about forty-eight feet long. We covered the board with newsprint and ruled it off in twelve-inch squares. (I learned later that they should have been ten-inch squares.) There was no heat in the building, so we had to work with our coats on. All we had to work with was crayons, a couple of yardsticks and a steel tape, a piece of twine and a nail for a compass, and a long flexible strip of wood that served as a straightedge one way, and bent the other way formed a sort of adjustable French curve to smooth up contours for the roof, front and back decks and fenders. A pocket protracter combined with a makeshift plumb bob helped check angles with reasonable accuracy.

To help decide on various dimensions we had a Cadillac, a Packard and an Oldsmobile to start, and later brought in a Ford and a Chevrolet, and we went over the cars part by part to find which measurements looked the best for the body style we wanted, and would still allow plenty of room inside. The production man was big, over six feet tall, and anything that fit him comfortably should be big enough for anybody, so he climbed in and out of the cars while we checked measurements and, one by one, transferred them to the board.

Helping with the measurements, and holding one end of the wood strip, was Herman Ringling, an old-time body knocker Tucker knew at the Speedway and who later masterminded the job of transferring the body from sketches directly to metal, without any kind of a model. A quiet, unobtrusive, rather mousy little man, Herman could do things with cold sheet metal that few other men could have done with a torch. In his field he was an artist, and a master.

There were plenty of problems to be solved, and if the answers weren't right it would really foul things up later. Decisions which had to be made included the angle of the windshield and the distance between the windshield and the driver's head; height and size of the back window; foot space in front and rear compartments, and the angle of the toe boards.

Front seats were standard height, twelve to thirteen inches, which governed height of the steering wheel from the floor, and the depth and angle of the front seat affected the angle of the wheel. One feature that was determined then was the step-down frame. The production man squawked his head off, but measurements showed it was the only way to stay within sixty inches overall height with standard front seats, and without sacrificing road clearance.

The dimensions set up at this time were, with few exceptions, the ones that were used in the final body design. There was no great attempt at styling, though the side silhouette was nearly identical with the finished design. An extra four inches were allowed on wheelbase, because Tucker was still insisting on fenders that turned with the wheels, and the production man said there would be plenty of time to talk him out of that later.

We did three views—top, front and side—all actual size, and the whole job took less than a week. It was too cold to dawdle and the quickest way to get warm was to finish up and get out.

On Christmas Eve in 1946, Tucker commissioned Alex Tremulis to do a styling job. Tremulis was fresh out of the Air Force and working for a Chicago product design and engineering company, but his first love was automobiles, and in Tucker he saw a chance to get back into automobile design. Slender, of medium height, Tremulis looked like an artist, which he was, with occasionally a temperament to match. Usually, he appeared a bit disheveled, with rumpled hair, as if he just got up from the drawing board after wrestling with some design problem. When he talked about automobiles he suddenly came to life, with a wealth of fascinating experiences and endless ideas for some change in fender or hood lines, or some ultramodern conception that was farther ahead than moon rockets. Friendly and communicative, Tremulis at the same time was excitable, and might flare up at criticism as if it were a personal affront.

Before the war he had been chief stylist for Auburn, Cord and Duesenberg at Connersville, Indiana, and had designed several racing cars including an ultra-streamlined job for Ab Jenkins. A week earlier he had phoned Tucker at the plant asking for an appointment, and Tucker told him he could have fifteen minutes.

"I showed him a three-quarter perspective of what I thought the automobile should look like," Tremulis said, "and he was tremendously impressed.

"Then I showed him some of my other designs—stuff I had done for Cord and Duesenberg, and sketches I had made while I was in the Air Force, my ideas of what the 'Postwar Car' should be. Before I left we spent three hours talking about design, and he told me what he didn't like about the designs he already had, and explained some of the features he wanted.''

Christmas Eve Tremulis came to Tucker's apartment in the Drake Hotel where a crowd of Tucker people was waiting to see the new sketches. He opened a large folder and held the drawings up, one and two at a time. Tucker asked the rest how they liked them. Nearly everybody hesitated, watching Tucker; when it was clear he liked them there came a roar of applause.

I liked all except the front fenders which I thought stunk, and said so. My popularity couldn't have dropped faster with a sudden attack of smallpox. Tucker scowled at me for a week, though much later he admitted that at least he agreed with my logic.

I thought the front fenders were a jarring note in an otherwise classic design, but Tucker liked them and so, apparently, did the public which after all is the final arbiter of styling, whether it's automobiles or exposed cleavage. One writer described them poetically as ''curved like the half-folded wings of a hovering bird,'' and said the front bumper looked ''like the horns of a Texas steer.''

Tucker suggested some changes and then told Tremulis to get going, he was in a hurry. So Tremulis took the drawings home and started work on new sketches that same night. He used most of the measurements on the full-scale layouts we had done in the plant, and from them started new drawings that were scaled accurately. Six days later he called Tucker and said the sketches were ready, and when could he come to look at them?

''It was about seven o'clock New Year's Eve when he got to our office in the Field Building, on his way to a party,'' Tremulis said. ''He looked at the pictures and told me:

'' 'That's it.'

''Nobody could have been more surprised than I was, because all I intended them for was preliminary sketches. But he said, 'First thoughts are the best,' and I think now he was right. The job was finished in five working days, and I think it was the fastest styling job that was ever done.

''I'm sure it was the fastest job ever done of making a full-size metal prototype of a production car directly from draw-

Prismatic Ward

1 ☀

Enchant Creature

When Prismatic Ward comes into play, choose a color; all damage dealt to target creature by sources of that color is reduced to 0.

"These, of all spells, must have common components I can isolate and use." —Halvor Arensson, Kjeldoran Priest

Illus. L. A. Williams

OLD NAVY CLOTHING CO. - 5553
161 WASHINGTON AVE. EXT.
ALBANY NY. 12205
Tel. (518)464-9502
05/23/98

5553-01 SALE   12:05 028   155

    GIFT CERT ISSUED   40.00
         # 000233107434

0

        TOTAL   40.00

        CASH TENDERED   40.00
        CHANGE   .00

FOR LOCATIONS CALL 1-800-OLD-NAVY

THANK YOU - OLD NAVY CLOTHING CO.
FOR LOCATIONS CALL 1-800-OLD-NAVY

RETURN/EXCHANGE POLICY

IF YOU ARE NOT SATISFIED WITH YOUR PURCHASE, SIMPLY BRING IT BACK WITHIN 30 DAYS, ALONG WITH YOUR RECEIPT, FOR A FULL REFUND OR EXCHANGE. ITEMS RETURNED AFTER 30 DAYS, WITH A RECEIPT, WILL RECEIVE A MERCHANDISE CREDIT FOR THE AMOUNT OF PURCHASE. ITEMS RETURNED WITHOUT A RECEIPT WILL RECEIVE A MERCHANDISE CREDIT FOR THE CURRENT SELLING PRICE. WE RESERVE THE RIGHT TO LIMIT QUANTITIES PURCHASED.

RETURN/EXCHANGE POLICY

IF YOU ARE NOT SATISFIED WITH YOUR PURCHASE, SIMPLY BRING IT BACK WITHIN 30 DAYS, ALONG WITH YOUR RECEIPT, FOR A FULL REFUND OR EXCHANGE. ITEMS RETURNED AFTER 30 DAYS, WITH A RECEIPT, WILL RECEIVE A

ings without a clay model. Beginning New Year's Eve, the model was ready for paint in one hundred days.''

Tucker told Tremulis he was chief stylist as of New Year's Eve.

There was still a shortage of modeling clay. We tried other automobile companies, but couldn't pry enough loose from anybody to even start work on a clay mockup.

"We don't need clay," Tucker said confidently. "Herman Ringling can make anything if you just show him the pictures. Try it and you'll find out."

So Tremulis went out into the shop where Ringling and another metal man started beating on sheet iron, cutting and welding. Another man on the job was Al McKenzie, former racing mechanic on the Horace Dodge boats.

On clay models a wooden form roughly the shape of the car, called a "buck," is used for the base, adding clay to fill in the body shape and smooth out the many contours. Going directly to metal they still needed some place to start, so they used an Oldsmobile for a sort of "body buck," starting with comparison measurements to locate the seats, doors, dash and other parts.

As each part of the new Tucker body was finished the original part from the Olds was junked, so when they got through about the only parts that remained from the original body were the roof, which had been completely reshaped, and door handles, window mechanisms, locks and hardware—parts that were the same whether they came from another automobile or from the manufacturer's bins.

The first car was, of course, completely handmade, and nobody connected with the job ever claimed it wasn't. It also had plenty of solder, probably several hundred pounds. Maybe Cellini could have hammered out a body in ten years without using solder, but nobody in his right mind would try it on a one-shot job where one of the most important factors was speed. The one-piece windshield had to be abandoned because they couldn't get curved glass except on special order, with no assurance they could even get it later.

Perhaps another twenty bodies were made with preliminary hardwood forms, but the rest were stamped out with metal dies and the body parts probably were about as good as any in the industry.

Many of the design ideas were Tucker's. While Tremulis persuaded him to forget the turning fenders, Tucker still insisted on doors opening into the roof, over the anguished protests of body men, who said it would raise production cost and weaken the roof. When one car rolled over in tests there was no indication of roof failure, but it unquestionably increased production cost. A typical Tucker touch was a narrow ledge just above the toe board in front, on the passenger side. If a man wanted to lie back and rest he could hook his heels on the ledge, and be comfortable. The center headlight, while not original, was Tucker's idea, as were the six exhausts extending out below the rear bumper.

Always a perfectionist where automobiles were concerned, Tucker wasn't satisfied that the first body was as good as it could be, so he hired a design firm from the east, Lippincott & Margulies, to do a clay model. By the time they started clay was finally available. They scraped, kneaded and patted clay for months with agonizing slowness, while everybody but Tucker fumed.

"They worked on that model several months, and when they got through the only part of their design that was used was the two taillight castings," Tremulis said. "They were undoubtedly the most expensive taillights in automotive history."

Tremulis continued as chief stylist, working on changes for future models, and had body No. 57 when the plant closed down.

"We were changing the rear window to a full wrap-around and had already started to cut out openings for the re-styling job," he said. "We were also planning changes in the front fenders which we were going to experiment with on that body. There were other minor changes such as any automobile company works on continuously to keep their styling up to date."

Tremulis later had the satisfaction of proving, to himself at least, that his design would be recognized instantly as a Tucker and nothing else.

With another Tucker man driving, he was going to Des Moines to show a car at a meeting of the SAE (Society of Automotive Engineers). Crossing the Mississippi River at

Clinton, Iowa, they didn't see the sign for the toll house on the Illinois side and were stopped by a motorcycle policeman halfway across the bridge.

"I'm sorry," said the driver. "We didn't see it. We'll go on across and turn around."

"No you won't," said the cop. "You passed the toll house without paying and you'll back up and pay."

It was a two-lane bridge, and Tremulis said traffic was really getting fouled up, so he asked the cop if it wouldn't be easier just to go across and make a U-turn.

The cop wasn't arguing.

"I've heard all about these Tuckers that can't back up," he said. "Now you just back right up to the toll house and pay up."

So they backed halfway across the bridge and paid the twenty-five-cent toll.

"Well I'll be damned," said the cop as he waved them on.

Here was one of the first Tuckers in operation. And it had to meet the lies spread about it by enemies, that it could not back up. It nailed that lie to the floor the first time out.

12

The Tin Goose

BY THE TIME THE NEW BODY WAS WELL ALONG, WITH EVERY new part making it look more like an automobile, the franchise program was going strong and there was money in the bank for the first time since the corporation started.

Rockelman announced that more than one hundred dealers had been signed in twenty-one states, including thirty-six in Illinois and eighteen in North Carolina. Garavito was back in business at 39 Pearl Street in New York's financial district, and had negotiations in the works for Mexico, Central and South America and parts of Europe, Asia and Africa.

The wonderful Tin Goose was about to be born.

And high time, too, because the body needed a chassis to hold it up. Nobody knows how the name "Tin Goose" got started, but it was used affectionately by the boys working on it. The first Tri-Motor airplane, built for Ford by Bill Stout, also was called the Tin Goose.

If Tucker thought he had troubles before, he soon realized that they were just a workout. His new troubles were engineers.

There is something about teaching a man to operate a slide rule that gives him a God complex, with overtones of Einstein. Even when the answer is off a few decimals one way or the other, as frequently happens, the slide-rule superman will brush it off with lofty disdain: what's a decimal, after all? I got the answer without using a pencil and paper like ordinary people, didn't I?

Within the broad classification of mechanical engineers there are various sub-species, which can be divided roughly into two groups: Monkey Wrench Engineers, who drive their wives to despair because with no warning at all they turn up greasy and unpresentable, and Paper Engineers, who are clean and neat and look like the models in *Esquire* magazine.

The monkey-wrench boys have an unquenchable curiosity to find out if their ideas will actually work, and can be found nights and weekends smeared with grease from eyebrows to shoelaces, completely happy. If their nails look grimy when company drops in, to hell with the company. Paper engineers don't give a damn if they never find out whether their ideas are any good or not. Their philosophy is let the jerks with money work on it.

At the Tucker plant the monkey wrench engineers were probably outnumbered two to one. The stable of prima donnas in the engineering department made Rudolph Bing's divas look like a *kindergesang* in Milwaukee. With a few exceptions, each engineer believed the rest were a lot of dopes and if Tucker just listened to him, he'd have an automobile.

Tucker had some screwy ideas just as Henry Kaiser did and, like Kaiser, he insisted that his engineers try to work them out. Basically his approach was the same as in any big company, in which standard practice is to toss a lot of engineers in the pot, keep it stirred up and hope something useful comes out.

Naturally, a few engineers did know their business, and these few finally built one hell of an automobile, in spite of red tape and the endless procession of expects that cluttered up the drafting rooms. But that was after the Tin Goose. The job now was to translate Tucker's ideas into displacement and horsepower, gears and bearings, and castings and forgings.

* * *

Tucker's overall design was basically sound, and the controversy at the time over front versus rear-engine placement was silly, as has been proved by countless thousands of highly successful rear-engine cars and buses operating today. The main obstacle to any manufacturer's switching to rear engine was the cost of a complete retooling job, running easily into millions of dollars. Tucker said conventional American automobiles were "front heavy," that front wheels had to carry most of the braking load, and the rear end didn't have enough weight for traction. Chrysler backed up his arguments on brakes when it put heavy double-cylinder brakes on its front wheels.

Tucker's arguments for a rear engine were chiefly (1) combining power and weight where the power is applied, which is at the rear wheels except in front-drive cars; (2) better braking due to the shift of weight to the front when brakes are applied, and (3) a flat passenger compartment without a tunnel for the driveshaft, or a big bulge where the transmission sticks out. Drivers of Tucker cars today will endorse all three claims with enthusiasm. When you give a Tucker too much throttle on a standing start, they say, you may shear an axle but you won't hear the screech of tires shedding rubber as in some of the latest super-powered jobs out of Detroit.

Arguments against the rear engine were chiefly not enough weight in front, for steering, and cutting down on luggage space. The most important advantage of placing the engine in front is that it fits between the front wheels, where the space is so narrow (to allow room for the wheels to turn) that it isn't much good for anything else anyway. This also is an advantage of a straight, or "V" engine; it fits easily between the front wheels, where a flat or opposed engine might be crowded. As to luggage space, one writer commented: "It's debatable whether we need the vast and echoing caverns that mark many current cars."

Volkswagen, Porsche and Renault beat the weight problem by placing the front floor board and foot pedals between the wheels, moving the weight of passengers forward. VW has a large luggage compartment behind the rear seat, but it's awkward to reach. There have been many highly successful rear-engine cars, all foreign until the Corvair; others include the Czech Tatra and certain models of Isotta-Fraschini, Mercedes-Benz and Fiat, in addition to thousands of rear-engine buses on American highways today.

Design of the engine was likewise basically sound. Tucker wanted low rpm with high torque, and he decided a big engine was the answer. The first engine (in the Tin Goose), later called a "monstrosity," was 5 × 5: five-inch bore and five-inch stroke, with 589 cubic inches displacement, which gave it the name "589." Size of the engine alone didn't make it a monstrosity, nor did its potential power. It was a flat, or opposed engine that fit easily into a space 48 inches long, 24 inches wide and 17 inches high, complete with accessories.

Tucker was shooting for 150 horsepower which the engine would have delivered at 1,800 rpm. At the speed of modern engines it should have delivered around 300 horsepower, which perhaps made it a monstrosity in 1947 but isn't at all out of line with present auto power plants. At the slower engine speed it should have run 200,000 miles without a valve or ring job.

In the overall design, the one important feature that engineers couldn't beat was the double torque drive directly to the rear wheels. Tucker's plan called for placing the engine transversely between the wheels, with ends of the crankshaft coupled directly to the wheels, with variable pitch torque converters which would have vanes that could be swung across center to get reverse without gears.

This, said Tucker, would eliminate the transmission and differential. While this feature was a complete fiasco, it wasn't quite as fantastic as many charged at the time. One company in Detroit was reported recently to be testing two torque converters geared to the driveshaft to turn the rear wheels, which of course would eliminate the differential. Parsons, Tucker's vice president in charge of engineering, says the next logical step for Buick's variable pitch turbine is to turn the blades still farther and get reverse—without gears, as Tucker planned it.

Responsibility for publicizing and trying to incorporate this feature was chiefly Tucker's, as he continued to insist on it long after engineers found that there wasn't room enough for more than a single converter on each side, and that one converter big enough to do the job would be larger than the wheels. One irreverent suggestion left the engineers fuming—that they forget about the rear wheels and just put tires on the torque converters.

One more publicized feature was sound in theory, but ahead of its time. This was the business of spraying cylinder walls of the aluminum block with bronze, which Tucker said would have close to the same coefficient of expansion as the aluminum pistons and make closer tolerances possible. They tried it but the results weren't at all happy. Later Porsche chrome-plated aluminum cylinder walls with essentially the same result, and Porsche today has almost a monopoly in speed and endurance runs in its class.

About the only criticism of the body was that it had 600 pounds of solder, which was possible but unlikely. Plenty of solder was used, for the same reason they used an Oldsmobile body for a seat buck when they started building the model— it saved time and got the job done.

All this work was done under terrific pressure to get the job done fast. Not enough test equipment had been set up to go at it scientifically, and even if there had been there wasn't time to give it the standard research treatment that any new design needs. Tucker needed an automobile, and fast.

Much has been written about the "589" engine, and it may have been potentially all that was claimed for it. But for Tucker's purpose it had too many imperfections and by the time the World Premier was scheduled it was too late to change.

Final responsibility for failure of the engine-to-wheels torque converters was Tucker's, for it was he who insisted on this feature in the prototype. But for mechanical details of the engine and suspension he relied on his engineers, who had told him in effect: "Here's an engine with fuel injection that will do the job, and here's the suspension." Tucker said okay, let's make 'em.

Misplaced decimals may have been responsible for major defects in the first engine and suspension. It could have been that the job was rushed too fast, or mistakes were made in machining or assembly. Whatever the cause, the failure of various self-styled experts to get results, and the constant bickering and red tape in higher levels of the engineering and production departments, influenced the course of the corporation from that time on.

Tucker began to rely more and more on his own judgment in making decisions, and to concentrate important engineering work under small groups of monkey wrench engineers, under conditions in which they could work without having to get a purchase order and seven carbons every time they needed a stove bolt.

Thus the Tin Goose was born in an atmosphere of trial and error, hoopla and hurry-up. It was a stubborn child. It did not live up to its parents' expectations. But it showed flashes of genius as well as temperament, and to Tucker, it was a step in the right direction.

13

The Big Buildup

THE TIN GOOSE WOULD MEET CERF'S CONDITION THAT Tucker have "the semblance of a car" and he already had the plant, if he could persuade War Assets to go along with him until he put over the stock sale.

Tucker's agreement with WAA required that he have at least $15,000,000 cash by March 1. On February 26, less than a week before the deadline, WAA extended the time to July 1, conceding that he couldn't possibly have raised the money while he was fighting with Wyatt.

In a statement announcing extension of the deadline, Tucker said a registration statement for four million shares of common stock, at $5 a share, would be ready to file within the next week or so. When the first hassle with SEC ended around the middle of January, the commission was out in the cold; it had no authority over the corporation's affairs. But this situation did not last long, and it is highly improbable that SEC ever stopped its investigation, knowing Tucker would have to register his stock and would be right back again facing the bright lights and answering questions.

"Once its jurisdiction had been restored," said a report issued later, "the Commission promptly authorized a private investigation to determine whether stop order proceedings should be instituted under Section 8 (d) of the Securities Act."

Even after SEC cleared the stock it would still have to be sold, and that promised to be a problem. If Tucker could have put it on the market while he was still something of a public hero he wouldn't have had too much trouble, but the fight with Housing had cost him a lot in time and prestige, and a lot of people thought he was already out of business.

Publicity had built Tucker up into a national figure, but his free publicity ride was slowing down. There had been so many headlines that the newspapers were getting tired of him, and many felt it was time he stopped talking and started doing something. Actually he was doing far more than either the public or the papers knew, but it wasn't news. Now, with his prestige at an all-time low, he knew Cerf could never put over a $20,000,000 issue without help.

At this point, Roy S. Durstine entered the picture. Durstine had his own advertising agency in New York, where he formerly was the Number 3 man in the famous Batten, Barton, Durstine and Osborn organization, and became one of advertising's immortals through handling of the Serutan account, one of the first to use the device of spelling something backwards.

Durstine was brought in by John Jenkins, Tucker's friend on the *Chicago Daily News,* and with Durstine came Ellis J. Travers, former associate of Jenkins. Travers had been advertising manager of Nash at Kenosha, Wisconsin, in the early days when most of the auto companies were bursting with money. After more than fifteen years with Nash he went to Detroit with Ruthrauff and Ryan, national agency handling some of the Chrysler accounts. In the new Durstine setup Travers was vice president and manager of the Chicago office, and Jenkins, also a vice president, headed the publicity department.

But even with Durstine manning the guns there were still problems, because during what SEC calls the "incubation period"—from the time stock is registered until it is cleared for sale—no advertising is permitted. And even after the stock is cleared, the stock itself can't be advertised except through what the trade calls "tombstone" ads, restrained and dignified notices in newspaper financial sections, usually enclosed in heavy black rule like obituary notices.

There maybe neophytes, inhabitants of the hushed inner temples of SEC in Philadelphia, who believe that stock is sold by this kind of advertising, but people experienced in business and finance—which includes the upper echelons of SEC—know that stock is sold just like any other commodity from toothpaste to foreign policy; by beating the drums and telling the public what a terrific bargain it is getting.

While SEC can't officially permit stock to be advertised, unofficially it takes a more realistic position, because without some kind of promotion very little stock would ever be sold and most new business would be dead before it even got started, and this eventually would put SEC out of business. So it permits advertising during a stock issue as long as the stock itself isn't advertised, thus getting around the law while technically observing it.

Theoretically SEC bans advertising "stressing the merits of the manufacturer's product" during the stock-selling period, though how a manufacturer can advertise without stressing the merits of his product may seem a trifle obscure.

The fact is that few companies suspend advertising during a stock issue, and advertising their product can be expected to stimulate the sale of their stock. So the normal procedure would be to intensify advertising before and during an issue, and back it up with press releases and other forms of unpaid publicity, over which SEC doesn't have much control.

Appointment of Durstine was announced February 24, and shortly afterward he set up the Chicago operation in the traditional grand manner of any agency that takes on an important new account in a city where it doesn't have a branch office. Plush quarters were opened in the Civic Opera building and almost everybody except the office help was a vice president. More personnel was added, including copy writers, an art director and artists and another publicity man, and the mill was ready to start grinding.

Durstine went to work trying to repair Tucker's damaged reputation, and started national advertising with full-page ads the first week in March. The body for the Tin Goose was already well along, and with it and Tremulis' sketches they finally had good art work for the first time. Copy in the ad told an exciting story.

"You'll get the motoring thrill of your life," the ad said. "You'll find nothing you've experienced before will compare with the smooth surge of FLOWING POWER from the Tucker *rear engine* drive . . . the new comfort of riding on the unique Tucker individual wheel suspension . . . the feeling of security you have in driving a car so precisely balanced that it almost drives itself."

After the heading "Here's the Success Story of America's most exciting Motor Car," short paragraphs reviewed Tucker's background, describing the plant and listing top executives, and below was a picture of the car captioned: "THE NEW TUCKER . . . YEARS AHEAD!"

People close to the operation agreed that Durstine did a good job, considering the chronic state of crisis. About the only valid criticism was that on occasion he let Tucker get his neck out too far in some of the advertising, and perhaps encouraged him to spend too much money.

But it wasn't the usual situation of an agency scheduling an over-heavy advertising program to collect its 15 percent, because for the time and work involved Durstine didn't make any great amount of money. Going overboard on shows and advertising could be credited largely to Travers, who always before had worked with companies which had plenty of money and could afford to do things in a big way. This technique had worked in the past and Travers depended on it to work again. He had been wiped out in the '29 crash, and he was trying for a comeback. Tucker looked like the answer, and he used every trick in his book to make Tucker's advertising pull its share of the weight.

Travers was thin, nervous and exacting. If he needed an artist, it had to be the highest priced artist he could find, and when they hired models they had to be off the top layer in the model agency's stable.

His action after taking over the account also was in the best tradition of big business and advertising. In a short time he had double-crossed everybody who had had a part in building Tucker up to where he was when Durstine came in. There was no particular malice in this, for Travers himself was rather a nice guy. It seemed rather that he had been operating that way so long he had forgotten there was any other way, and it had become a conditioned reflex.

Over the entire period with Tucker, Durstine scheduled around $800,000 in advertising, which wasn't excessive for the length of time involved. It can't be denied that much of the advertising was unnecessary, but whether the responsibility was Travers', Tucker's or a combination of the two was anybody's guess.

Since advertising had to be called off until the stock finished incubating, Durstine concentrated on the World Premiere which was scheduled for June 19. The Premiere had two purposes: to show the Tucker to dealers and distributors, who were clamoring to see the car they had put up money to handle, and to impress brokers who would be selling the stock.

The World Premiere also was timed to give the stock issue a healthy shot in the arm after the sale was well under way, which under the commission's normal twenty-day waiting period would be on or around March 26. So now all Tucker had to do was get ready for the Premiere and wait for the green light from SEC.

14

Off to Philadelphia

IF THERE HAD BEEN ANY QUESTION OF WHAT SEC INTENDED to do, it was soon answered. After an eight-day private investigation, the commission issued a Stop Order and set June 11 for a public hearing. Tucker was in the headlines again, but not the kind of headlines he needed. Tucker saw another delay coming up, and it could be fatal.

This action was neither entirely unexpected nor particularly unusual. Stop orders are an occupational hazard, what Tucker called "standard equipment." Cerf's contract included a clause in which the company agreed to use its best efforts to prevent a stop order from being issued and, if issued, to "secure the lifting of such order at the earliest possible moment."

The stop order automatically moved opening of the stock sale ahead another twenty days, which put Tucker right back in the soup with War Assets, because he didn't have a chance in the world of meeting the July 1 deadline.

One of the chief reasons for the stop order was SEC's objection to what seemed a devious way of paying $8,750 to

Abraham Karatz, who had worked with Tucker on original promotion of the deal and had been squeezed out some months earlier by some of Tucker's associates. Payment to Karatz didn't show in the company's prospectus, which violated the provision calling for "full disclosure."

The fact that Karatz had done time didn't bother Tucker who, as a former cop, reasoned that he had served his time and the slate was clean. But when the time came for selling the stock, some on the board of directors felt that Karatz' record might pop up at an embarrassing moment, and insisted that he had to go.

SEC said Cerf had put the finger on Karatz. Cerf said he had nothing to do with it. Whoever was responsible, Karatz reluctantly changed his name to Harold H. Karsten and was banished to Los Angeles, where Tucker promised to keep him eating until cars were in production and he could take over a distributorship. From exile Karatz occasionally wired encouragement and congratulations to the company signed "Harold," which he thought was a huge joke. Tucker told SEC:

"He wants a dealership out West someplace and I'll see that he gets it."

Tucker was in the middle. He had made certain commitments to Karatz that he wanted to keep, and at the same time he had to get along with his board. So Karatz had been paid off indirectly by one of Tucker's press agents and his "B" stock was held by a dummy. While use of dummies was neither new nor uncommon, coupled with Karatz' record it proved to be a mistake.

Not that it was a mistake to work with Karatz in the first place, because he was competent, tireless in his enthusiasm and entirely cooperative, with endless patience. During early days of the deal he was on call twenty-four hours a day answering phones, running errands, taking care of detail and picking up and delivering big wheels at the airport. No job was too big or too small for him, from finding a public stenographer on a Sunday morning to entertaining visiting VIPs when Tucker was tied up. Most of the people who worked with Karatz at the time liked him, except for a few professional Aryans who would automatically have hated anybody named Karatz or Goldberg.

My only complaints with Abe were that he was a lousy driver and he snored. Most of us after one trip would grab the wheel first, which was fine by him because he didn't particularly like to drive anyway. Tucker recruited some of the top snoring virtuosos of all time and Abe was high on the list. One night in Washington we were billeted together at the Mayflower at a time even the flop joints were booked weeks in advance. Abe was in exceptionally good voice, and about two in the morning I gave up and moved my mattress and pillow into the closet. I almost smothered but finally got to sleep.

Karatz unquestionably had earned a place on the payroll for helping get the deal started, and likewise had earned a slice of the "B" stock that went to others who were in on the initial stages. Tucker had told Karatz he would take care of him but Karatz wanted a firm agreement in writing. He knew he couldn't trust the board when it came time to collect on the promises. So he got himself a lawyer and threatened to sue.

Easing Karatz out of the deal without taking care of him was a mistake, because this controversy was one of the more messy details in the Philadelphia hearing and didn't reflect any great credit on the *goyim*.

The day before the hearing a mob of Tucker people came down like locusts on the staid Warwick Hotel in Philadelphia. Haughty matrons glared at the noisy intruders from the dining room, where they were gathering strength for a new assault on Wanamakers. Tucker arrived at the last minute in the twin-engine Beechcraft, bought from the Walgreen Drug Company a short time before.

Karatz was there with his attorneys, and throughout the night messengers ran back and forth between the two camps trying to arrange a compromise. Tucker wanted to go along but his attorneys would have no part of it. They could have been merely protecting their own future position, because they screamed as only lawyers can scream when it looks as if their tail will be caught in the door instead of the client's.

When it finally was straightened out to SEC's satisfaction, the prospectus detailed payments made to Karatz and gave him another billing under "Litigation." The prospectus stated

Karatz' claim that Tucker personally had promised him a southern California distributorship and 100,000 shares of "B" stock. Other threatened lawsuits included Granik's.

The argument with SEC lasted two days and closed when the commission acceded to Tucker's request that they dispense with the customary report from the trial examiner, and waive the briefs and oral arguments which usually follow. How long they might deliberate was anybody's guess.

By this time Senator Ferguson was back in the act with his Senate Surplus Property committee, demanding that WAA throw Tucker out of the plant on his head the exact minute the July 1 deadline expired if he didn't have the $15,000,000. One WAA official told Ferguson that Tucker "would have to put up or get out by July 1," so Ferguson backed off. Another official on Tucker's side revealed that he had already paid WAA $600,000, of which $200,000 was back rent and the balance a "good faith" deposit.

SEC could have knocked Tucker out then by delaying its ruling until after July 1, when Ferguson probably would be able to put enough pressure on WAA to get Tucker thrown out of the plant. Tucker knew even better than Ferguson that if he lost the plant he could forget about the stock issue. So he took off for Washington in the Beech and started shooting angles again. He found one in a Senate subcommittee headed by Republican Senator George W. Malone of Nevada, who had been feuding with SEC for years over restrictions which he said were strangling new mining ventures in Nevada and other Western states. Malone saw a chance to take another swing at one of his favorite targets.

Within a few days Malone's committee called in SEC top officials to renew his complaint that SEC policies were "operating to discourage venture capital from flowing into new enterprise."

"There is considerable evidence that SEC is going beyond its legal authority in examining the financing of new ventures," Malone said, adding that his committee was interested in the Tucker case "as an example of how SEC operates."

A week after Malone's blast, on June 26, SEC cleared Tucker's stock, with another twenty-day waiting period which delayed opening of the sale to July 15. On the same day WAA moved the deadline ahead another four months to November 1.

The prospectus, as finally amended and cleared by SEC, painted a gloomy picture that would have scared the hell out of a wary investor. But for the average investor it might as well have been printed in Sanskrit, because most people read a prospectus less carefully than they do the fine print in an insurance policy. One SEC pronouncement said:

"The contrast between information contained in previous publicity and that in the prospectus, as it now has been amended, is so pronounced that we deem it necessary to warn the investing public of the danger of relying on any past judgment . . . in determining whether to purchase the securities of the registrant."

SEC makes a big issue of not "approving" a stock, and just mentioning the word can start even a minor employee on a routine that sounds like a tape recording. He will explain that SEC does *not* approve, or pass on the merits or any security offered, that it only *permits* a stock to be sold after it is satisfied that full disclosure has been made. But the distinction is largely academic, because to the average Joe the stock is approved when it is cleared, and there isn't a thing SEC can do about it.

In Tucker's case SEC not only did not approve the issue, it disapproved publicly and vociferously and at considerable length. It was now up to Tucker to convince the public that Tucker stock was a pretty darn good buy, no matter what SEC said about it. That was not easy to do.

In publicity, however, the company was in pretty good shape again. The World Premiere had gone off successfully as scheduled on June 19, while SEC was still deliberating, when it was too late to call it off even if they had wanted to. Even though the Premiere had been over almost a month when the stock sale began, it helped get the sale off to a good start, because months later people who saw the show were still talking about it.

_____ *15*

World Premiere

ALTHOUGH THE STOP ORDER WAS STILL IN EFFECT AND THERE was no indication when the stock could be sold, if at all, the World Premiere went off June 19 with no perceptible dampening of enthusiasm.

Invitations had been sent to 651 dealers and distributors to bring prospective dealers and guests, and replies indicated about 1,100 would attend. Special guests added another 1,200, plus 500 investment bankers invited by Cerf. With another 150 representatives from newspapers, magazines and radio stations, attendance was estimated at 3,000, which was the seating capacity of the factory assembly room where the show was set up.

Long before 9 o'clock in the morning, parking lots in front had filled up. By noon extra police were called to handle traffic on Cicero Avenue in front of the plant, and they estimated more than 5,000 persons came to see the show. There were more than 1,000 out-of-state cars and fifteen special buses.

Travers was an old hand at putting on shows and this was

108

one of his best efforts. One of the prettiest girls in the plant presided at the reception desk, and costumed page girls took the guests to regional registration desks where they received badges and programs. As soon as people registered they were lined up for tours through the plant. Motorized trains with open-seat cars ran continuously until noon.

Lunch was served cafeteria style in the main cafeteria and two dining rooms, and there was no dallying over coffee because the multitudes had to eat in shifts. By 3 o'clock everybody had been fed and ushers herded the mob into the assembly room. Ceiling-high blue and silver drapes covered one stage with a turntable, and another smaller stage near the wall.

After a fanfare from the band, Rockelman called the meeting to order and the band started the National Anthem. Four Marine color bearers in summer uniforms marched down the aisles and stood at attention after raising the colors on the stage. After the invocation by a Chicago minister, Rockelman introduced special guests and made a short talk, explaining to dealers that they were in a "virtual partnership proposition," because dealers' and distributors' money, together with investments by Tucker and his associates, had made early financing of the corporation possible.

"We are all in this together and we are here today not only to see the car itself, but to learn of the progress that the corporation has made," Rockelman said.

Next speaker was Tucker, who outlined the background and history of the corporation, including the first altercation with SEC over franchise sales, the fight with the Housing Administration and the current battle to get the stop order lifted so sale of stock could be started. Other officials followed Tucker at the microphone, droning on and on until the crowd began to get restless. They had come to see the car, not listen to a lot of guff about what great guys all the Tucker officials were.

If some people in the audience thought things seemed a bit disorganized, they should have seen the madhouse backstage, where tired mechanics who had worked all night were still laboring to get the car ready in time for the afternoon show.

The Tin Goose was a hurry-up job and Tucker, like Henry Kaiser, had insisted on certain features which later had to be abandoned. One of these was a 24-volt electrical system. The industry vindicated Tucker's judgment, that more powerful batteries were needed to operate all the gadgets, when it went to 12 volts within the next few years. But that didn't help any at the time, because the only standard equipment available, such as generators and starters, was 6-volt except for a few trucks which used 12-volt batteries.

The production department was dickering with various suppliers to furnish 24-volt batteries and equipment, so engineers solved the immediate problem by putting 24-volt airplane engine starters on the two engines, in the display car and the chassis. The big six-cylinder 5-by-5 engine needed plenty of push to turn it over, and the airplane starters had only a five-to-one power ratio compared to the standard 20-to-one on automobiles.

To start the cars for testing they used portable batteries on an electric truck, with a small battery in the car for ignition. But for the show the car had to start without outside help, so they put in two 12-volt truck batteries weighing 167 pounds each. The handmade body was already heavy with several hundred pounds of solder or more, and adding another 300 pounds of batteries was the last unbearable straw, putting too much extra weight on the rear end.

The first suspension arms were cast aluminum and too light for the job. During testing the arms held up all right and it wasn't until the morning of the show, after the two heavy truck batteries had been installed in the rear, that the arms collapsed.

Mechanics and test drivers rushing to get the car ready for the Premiere had enough on their minds without worrying about the suspensions, which had been passed by the engineering department. First problem was that the direct fuel injection system didn't work right. Solving this was simple: they just disconnected the system and installed twin carburetors on the intake manifolds.

The second and more serious trouble was the valve-actuating mechanism. The design was theoretically practical, using an activating pump that worked like a distributor, with oil lines to the valves, which were operated by hydraulic pressure instead of the standard push rods. But when the engine picked up speed and increased the oil pressure, air got in the oil lines and the timing went crazy. There being no quick remedy for this, they had to drive the car the way it was.

The first suspension arm broke about 10:30 in the morning with Ralph Hepburn, Western zone manager, driving. The arm was the right rear, and if it had broken five minutes earlier it probably would have killed two mechanics working on the valve-actuating mechanism. One of the mechanics was Dan Leabu, who had come to Chicago from Tucker's Ypsilanti plant.

"Charley Desmet and I were under the engine just before it broke," Leabu said. "It must have been about the third time that day we had bled the lines trying to get the valve timing back where it belonged. It was just luck we weren't underneath because we would have been squashed flat."

The arm was replaced and mechanics continued checking other parts. They were dirty and tired, but there would be no sleep until the car had been driven from the stage into a roped-off area in the assembly room.

About 1 o'clock in the afternoon both rear suspensions arms broke with the car just standing still, and then a front arm snapped. The men who had worked in the pits at Indianapolis didn't need to hold a conference when that happened. They rushed to the mechanic shop where four new arms of tough beryllium copper were machined from solid stock. One by one they were installed, while speakers in the assembly room kept talking to hold the audience until the car was ready.

It was almost 4:30 in the afternoon when the car was pushed up on the platform behind the drapes, and Tucker went backstage to receive the applause and congratulations of grinning, greasy mechanics. "Let's go," they told him. "What the hell are we waiting for?" Waiting models touched up their makeup and took their positions. The real show was about to begin.

Four models in strapless evening gowns stepped out from behind the curtains and sounded a fanfare on long gold trumpets, and at a signal from Tucker other models stepped up and drew back the drapes.

There stood the car in full side view under a battery of spotlights, its rich maroon finish gleaming against the white shoulders of the models who towered above it. Only sixty inches high, it was the lowest passenger car built in the United States, and it was two inches longer than the largest Cadillac. After a brief pause the turntable began turning slowly, pausing every quarter turn to give the audience a look from every angle. People in the jammed assembly room went wild, shouting, whistling and cheering.

When the applause died down Tucker introduced his blond daughter Marilyn, then 20, who could have traded places with any of the models. Marilyn was to christen the car, and when the turntable stopped she grabbed the bottle of champagne and stepped up. The bottle was wrapped in fine wire netting so broken glass wouldn't puncture the tires when the car was driven off, but that didn't bother Marilyn. She took a lusty swing at the front bumper and champagne splashed all over the front of her father's suit, shirt and tie.

Anything that followed unveiling and christening of the car couldn't possibly be other than anti-climax, but what came next was still good showmanship. Nine more girls walked across the stage one at a time from behind the curtain, each carrying a part of a conventional automobile duplicated in papier mâché. Asked what they were carrying, the girls chirped, "A transmission from a conventional automobile," and so on. These were the parts Tucker said his car wouldn't need. Then another drape slid back, showing big conference tables piled high with letters and telegrams, part of more than 150,000 which had come in from all over the world after first publicity on the new Tucker automobile appeared.

Tucker made the final talk, which ended the formal portion of the afternoon session, and said in closing:

"Let's get one point straight. I want to build cars and make money, of course. But there's something else. This country has been good to me and I feel a debt of gratitude. I'd like to repay that debt, in part, by contributing something to America—something that will mean much to this country's future, an automobile that will mean truly safe, economical and comfortable transportation for millions of my countrymen."

After he finished Tucker introduced Hepburn, who started the car and drove it off the stage into the roped-off area where it stayed on display the rest of the afternoon. There, guards kept people from climbing over the ropes, and models added a decorative touch, while men from engineering and sales stayed by the car to explain design details to the curious. On the other stage were the chassis and various components of the automobile.

With the excitement over, people drifted out, some to go back home and others to their hotels to rest and freshen up for the night's activities in the Stevens Hotel, now the Conrad Hilton. The evening program started with a cocktail party in the swank Normandy Room, followed by a banquet and floor show in the grand ballroom.

While the show cost a lot of money it was immensely profitable to the corporation. Not many new franchises were signed because everybody was too busy, but many Tucker dealers who came in later had attended the preview and were tremendously impressed with the public's enthusiasm for the automobile, even though it wasn't demonstrated and there was no chance to examine it closely. The show was further profitable in that it carried public interest over the period from the stop order to opening of the stock sale July 15, and helped counteract the highly adverse publicity released by SEC with its announcement that the stock had been cleared.

And the show had one other result: it revealed dramatically to Tucker that something was haywire in his engineering department, and if the boys didn't produce some positive results over the next few months he had better start doing something about it.

But he had no time to worry about engineering then. The stock sale was set to open in less than a month. If the stock didn't sell there wouldn't be money to pay engineers anyway.

16

Colonel McCormick's Hat

ABOUT A WEEK AFTER THE STOCK SALE OPENED, TUCKER told me it wasn't going so good, and what could I do about it? I asked him:

"Pres, have you got one car that will run around the block without stopping?"

He said he didn't have a single car he could depend on. I told him there was little I could do, because without a new angle we couldn't even get local publicity, much less national. What the newspapers and wire services wanted now was actual demonstrations of the car.

But something had to be done and fast, so he called Durstine. SEC still frowned on advertising during the stock sale, but technically there was nothing wrong with showing the automobile. So Durstine went into action, and this began the series of shows held across the country, during which the Tin Goose piled up more mileage than any other automobile in the world without ever turning a wheel, except to run up and down the ramp of the Conestoga freight plane which Tucker bought later.

Since the trial the Tucker deal has become a classic example in college and high school economics classes to show how a fast operator can fleece the public with a worthless product, by putting on a ballyhoo and selling stock. Instructors seldom get an argument except from some kid whose parents own and drive a Tucker, or whose father was a dealer and drove a Tucker during demonstrations put on around the country.

It may come as something of a shock to economics teachers to learn that the public didn't batter down the doors of brokers' offices on the morning the stock sale opened, and that the public wasn't the pushover for Tucker stock that people have been led to believe. It took a lot of terrific work to sell even three fourths of the $20,000,000 issue by the time it was closed two months later.

Some shows had already been scheduled before the stock sale opened, but they received comparatively little publicity, partly because they came so soon after the Premiere. By far the most successful of these, for attendance and public enthusiasm, was the one put on at the New Products Exhibition, sponsored by the United Inventors and Scientists of America, in Los Angeles' big Pan-Pacific auditorium.

The car was flown out by the Flying Tigers and was on display one day when an emergency called it back to Chicago. There a showing had been set up in the Red Lacquer Room at the Palmer House for investment bankers, with a private preview earlier for the late Colonel Robert McCormick, publisher of the powerful *Chicago Tribune*.

Tucker had been hoping to get the Colonel on his side for a long time, because the *Tribune* was not only influential in Chicago but had a lot of weight in Washington too. Tucker finally succeeded in getting a commitment from the Colonel to come and see the car before the meeting for the investment bankers opened, and he had to get it back to Chicago fast.

In Los Angeles the Flying Tigers said the plane Tucker had chartered was on another flight and they refused to use another plane that was on the field. That put Tucker on the spot because he couldn't get the car back to Chicago overnight by rail. He looked at the plane on the field.

"How much?" he asked.

They told him $45,000, take it or leave it. Tucker took it; with millions at stake, $45,000 was small change. He called the auditorium to bring the car, and it was loaded and flown to Chicago.

From the airport the car was rushed to the Palmer House and jockeyed through the back entrance to a freight elevator. Jerry Thorp, then on the Durstine staff, was handling publicity on the show.

"I don't know how the hell they ever got it into the elevator," Thorp said. "Maybe they stood it on end. But they did, and they got it in place just three minutes before the Colonel arrived."

If Colonel McCormick had been bareheaded the demonstration might have changed the course of history. But he wore a hat and he was six feet four inches tall, and when he got in the front seat and straightened up his hat came down over his ears. He left shortly without comment, but from then on the *Tribune* played it pretty much down the middle. Tucker had made a good try, but circumstances were against him.

Back in Los Angeles the following day the exhibition set new attendance records and, with more than eighty exhibitors, the Tucker easily stole the show.

The odyssey of the Tin Goose is also the story of the Conestoga, which ended a short but active career in the mud beside the runway on a small Missouri airport, after a forced landing in a snowstorm.

From the side it resembled a hydrocephalic bug, with a bulging nose that was two floors high and a steep stairway connecting the lower compartment with the controls compartment on top. And as with a bug, all that held it together was its tough reinforced skin of stainless steel, which made it so heavy it was underpowered. New pilots would move the controls to put the ship in a bank and sit there wondering why nothing happened. It just took time. The Conestoga was clumsy but it was big—100-foot wing span and 68 feet long—

and it made an impressive prelude to a show when it came in for a landing.

While maximum cruising speed was listed at 186 miles an hour, pilots said it had one gait—it took off, flew and landed at 90—and except in an emergency they would never consider a runway under a mile long.

Pilots never trusted the Conestoga and never went up without parachutes. Most of them considered it pretty much of a dog, but it was a faithful dog and only threatened to quit once. This was on a return trip from Oakland, California, when the gauges for the left wing and nacelle tanks failed to work.

The only pilot who stayed with the ship was William A. (Bill) Denehie, who was flying with Bob Windette at 13,000 feet over Holbrook, Arizona, heading for Amarillo to take on gas. Windette, at the controls, told Denehie: "Take over. I'll go down and fix some coffee."

He took off his parachute, draped it over the seat and went down the stairs. Five minutes later, when he had his shoes off, getting ready to change clothes, he heard the left engine quit cold. Denehie flipped the crossover valve but nothing happened. They were losing altitude fast. Windette clawed his way up the stairway in his bare feet, and at the top he started putting on his 'chute.

"The hell with the parachute," Denehie yelled. "Get that auxiliary pump going!"

With the throttle wide open, the engine caught. They headed for Winslow, the nearest gas stop on the route, and there they had to wait until night for the air to become heavy enough for the plane to get off the runway.

At last report two Conestogas of the twenty or so that were built were owned by the Flying Tigers, and another had been abandoned and left in one corner of the airport at Mexico City.

Except for the Pan-Pacific show, which was handled by their own organization, Travers masterminded the shows and he gave them the same deluxe treatment as the Premiere. At one of the shows in New York Travers didn't like the models the agency sent over, priced at $50 each for the day.

"Are these the best you have?" he demanded. The agency man hastily assured Travers that their top string included the most beautiful girls in the world, but they would cost him $75. Travers said send them over, so the same girls came back with $75 price tags.

For stirring up public interest where there was money to buy stock, the show at the Museum of Science and Industry at Rockefeller Center in New York easily topped the entire list. There wasn't a door big enough to get the car through so they had to take out a window. The car was run inside on a Tuesday night in August, with the show scheduled to open Thursday.

Wednesday brought a typical Tucker riot. Carpenters and electricians were setting up the stage and turntable, and advertising people and models were running through a dress rehearsal when an excited attendant burst into the office of the museum director, Robert Shaw, without even stopping to knock.

"The place is mobbed," the attendant gasped. "Thousands of people hollering to get in."

The *New York Sun*, the only newspaper in New York to carry the announcement, had goofed, and it explained what happened later in a house ad under the caption "Was our face red!"

The newspaper ran the announcement with the wrong copy, which said "Opening Wednesday" instead of Thursday. Shaw had to let them in or call for help, so the rehearsal was postponed, workmen put the car in position on the unfinished stage and the doors were opened without any admission charge.

During the days that followed, the Tucker car outdrew every show on Broadway. *Variety* noted the event under the headline:

TUCKER AUTO, FIRST RUN
GETS BOFF 42 G IN N.Y.

Which, in translation, meant the Tucker car drew box office returns of $42,000 the first week. The story said:

"Broadway sho biz grosses may be caught in a downbeat, but the public evidently still has money to spend for an attraction if it's something it wants to see. That fact was pointed up sharply this week by the first public demonstration of the new Tucker automobile, which will gross an estimated $42,000 for the first seven days ending tomorrow. And, in all probability, will be held over an extra couple of days.

"Figure represents more than three times the average weekly grosses at the smaller Bway firstrun filmeries, such as the Globe, Gotham or Victoria. Tucker car, claimed to be the first one actually to incorporate modern postwar design, including an engine in the rear, has been playing to a average of 15,000 people daily at the New York Museum of Science and Industry in Radio City. Admission is a straight 48¢, including tax. Gross has been considered especially phenomenal in view of the fact that the display hasn't been advertised nearly so much as the average firstrun picture."

The nearest contender was Ethel Merman in "Annie Get Your Gun," which grossed $37,000 the same week for the first time since opening at the Imperial Theater, where previous receipts were never under $44,000.

The New Yorker gave the show more than two columns, largely adjectives, in its "Talk of the Town" section, describing Tucker as "a tall, handsome, clean-shaven, tight-lipped, curly-haired man wearing a dark blue suit and brown-and-white wing-tipped shoes . . . tailed by a retinue."

The show resembled the rest, with the car on a turntable and models adding a touch of glamour, and one incident the customers didn't see was in the best Tucker tradition. One of the announcers in the National Broadcasting Company upstairs heard about the exhibit and came down. Before the show started he crawled under the car to look at the engine, and while he was under somebody turned on the switch that started the turntable.

Tucker came down the aisle to open the show, in his lapel a carnation and on his arm Ginny Simms, who was currently thrushing at the Waldorf. Odd sounds seemed to be coming from somewhere inside the car, but Tucker couldn't see anything wrong. He went through his routine and left.

When the turntable finally stopped the disheveled announcer wormed his way out, somewhat scratched up but not seriously hurt.

Shaw said there were more than 100,000 paid admissions, with thousands of people coming to ask about the automobile during the ten-day showing. The exhibit was the idea of museum officials, who called Tucker and arranged to have the car brought to New York. Tucker got no part of the paid admissions and no attempt was made to sell either franchises or stock, though girls took the names of people who wanted further information, which was mailed to them. Shaw said people who saw the car were told clearly that it was a handmade prototype, and that certain changes would have to be effected before it could be put in production.

By using the Conestoga to make fast overnight jumps, the car was exhibited in most of the major cities in the United States and in Havana before the stock sale closed, and beyond any question it was an important factor in selling the stock. One of the first shows in the Chicago Arena drew more than 100,000 people, and at the Canadian National Exposition in Toronto the Tucker was a major attraction. Record crowds turned up in St. Louis and Boston, as shows followed in dizzy and bewildering succession.

The stock was barred in only two important states, Michigan and California. Tucker wasn't particularly surprised or bothered at being barred in Michigan, because he was already meeting opposition from the industry, which had strong representation in Lansing. But being barred in California was bad, because if the stock could have been sold there he probably would have raised the entire $20,000,000, so great was public interest following the Pan-Pacific show.

Tucker tried everything he could think of but he was never able to reach Governor Earl Warren personally, and the stock was still barred in California when the issue was closed. Early in September sales lagged so badly that Tucker told Cerf to call it off, and on September 12 Cerf handed Tucker a check for $15,007,000. This was the corporation's share after deducting commissions to Cerf and brokers who participated in the offering.

In a press release the same day, Tucker said the stock sale brought the cash position of the corporation to more than $17,000,000, in addition to some $2,000,000 in notes from distributors and dealers for franchises. The same day War Assets made Tucker's lease official in a telegram to the City National Bank in Chicago.

Tucker had gone a long way in less than two years. From a small office in Ypsilanti he had progressed to the world's biggest factory, with more than $17,000,000 cash and an automobile the public was ready to buy almost sight unseen.

Headlines, Headlines, Headlines . . .

WITH THE STOCK ISSUE CLOSED THERE WAS NO IMMEDIATE
need for more publicity, but it seemed as if some kind of
blood disease kept erupting in unpredictable spots. When one
inflamed area calmed down another would erupt, and they all
resulted in headlines.

A few days before the issue was closed there arose a story,
which must have circled the world in hours, that the Tucker
car wouldn't back up.

Ever since Colonel McCormick had bumped his head
against the top he had been wondering about reports that the
show car was a phony and wouldn't run. One day he called
Frank Sturdy, the *Tribune*'s automotive editor, and told him
to go out to the plant and do a story on the Tucker car, and
find out whether it would actually run.

Sturdy fought his way through one department after another, where people gave him the run-around, passed the buck
or refused to see him at all. He spent weeks trying to get the
interview set up, which didn't improve his disposition in the
least, and the Colonel was getting impatient. Finally a private

122

showing was arranged, handled personally by Lee Treese, vice president in charge of manufacturing, with Gene Haustein driving. Sturdy had to settle for a test chassis because the complete car was on display in Milwaukee.

Sturdy wrote a little more than a column with a two-column photograph, and the story was fair and reasonably favorable to the corporation except for one paragraph toward the end, under the subhead TEST CHASSIS CAN'T BACK UP. Considering the rough time they had given Sturdy they got off easy.

"The hydraulic torque converters on it are not equipped with a device to permit reversing," the story said. "Treese said a converter with a reversing method is being built."

It was true enough that the test chassis would not reverse and neither would the car, but it was neither bad engineering nor an oversight. The engineers were still trying to eliminate gears by using variable pitch vanes, and if the torque converters worked except for reverse, gears could be added. But there was no point in worrying about reverse gears until the torque converters proved out, so they simply didn't bother with it.

Tucker wasn't greatly concerned because he knew it was no problem, and he was a strong believer (at this time) in Henry Ford's philosophy, that if they spelled his name right he didn't care what they said about him. The story actually did no great harm, though dealers later said the first thing they had to do after they got a car was to back it up, because the public had heard the story and insisted on seeing for themselves.

The next story to make headlines was the resignation of Colonel Harry Aubrey Toulmin, Jr., as chairman of the board of directors. Toulmin was a patent attorney with offices in Dayton, and Tucker had met him while with Higgins in New Orleans. When Toulmin was elected chairman, Tucker hoped he would bring a more businesslike administration to the corporation. Tucker had neither the patience nor talent for the constant maneuvering and red tape of big business, and he counted on Toulmin to fill this gap.

The first handout announcing Toulmin's appointment said he was an officer or director in seven other corporations, the author of twenty books and holder of the Distinguished Service Medal and the Legion of Merit. The list of his citations, honors, and degrees filled more than two pages.

As befitted his position and background, Toulmin was impatient with the help and a bit on the pompous side, radiating an aura of executive importance. When he bailed out it was in the same grand manner, and he set a precedent for the exodus of executives that was to follow, holding a press conference in Dayton to tell the world he was leaving and what was wrong with the corporation and with Tucker personally.

Toulmin said he resigned "because Preston Tucker would not agree to my written demands that any money raised from the public should be spent and administered under the strictest regulation and controls normal to legitimate business.

The same afternoon in Chicago, Tucker told reporters that "not one cent of the $15,000,000 raised through the stock issue has been spent in any way," adding reasonably that it would be hard to get rid of that much money over the weekend. The issue had only closed the preceding Friday. Tucker added that part of the expenditures Toulmin was complaining about included $60,000 to his firm for patent work, with vouchers in process to bring the total up to around $73,000.

There was no question Toulmin had a point, even if he did jump the gun in protecting the stockholders, but Tucker had a point too. If he had to operate under the kind of regulations and controls Toulmin was accustomed to, he would never get anything done, because he had to move fast. And to move he had to push his board along with him, not drag along behind it.

Except for a few days of bad publicity Toulmin's resignation was no great loss, and to the general public it was an administrative squabble that was soon forgotten.

The last echoes of Toulmin's blast had barely died away when two more top officials were out, threatening legal action. They were Hanson Ames Brown, executive vice president, and James D. Stearns, treasurer and comptroller. Brown and Stearns, along with three minor executives, said they had been fired. Tucker said they resigned. Rockelman took over Brown's post.

In retrospect, the friction and final break between Tucker and most of his original group of experienced top-flight automotive men is no mystery, though at the beginning it could hardly have been foreseen and—even if foreseen—probably nothing could have been done about it.

Without exception, these men had worked with big established companies which had, for all practical purposes, all the time and money in the world. If a model cost twice as much to develop as originally estimated it created no great crisis, and if some new design remained in the works three years, there were still current models to fill in. When a new model was found to have some serious defects, or failed to go over with the public, as happened with almost every company at one time or another, they weathered the crisis, even when hundreds of cars had to be called in after they were sold to correct some defect.

With Tucker it was different—he had less than a year to develop and get ready for production an entirely new automobile, and only a limited amount of money with which to do it. The veterans with Tucker simply couldn't adjust. It was beyond them. It was completely outside their experience, and most of them were too old to change.

Without the names and prestige of these men, Tucker could never have sold his stock or even obtained the plant, but when the going got rough they were dead weight. So he turned immediately to the men he knew intimately, who were used to handling such problems as a matter of course. Problems were their business, and their life.

These were the men he had known at Indianapolis, who could design and build a complete racing car, with the precision of a fine watch, in less than a year, and make major repairs in a pit stop that would take weeks in an ordinary garage or repair shop.

The most important of these men, whom Tucker later made chief engineer, was Eddie Offutt, a quiet unassuming man who got things done, and wrote his memorandums after the job was finished. When Tucker first met him Offutt was a stocky man in his early 40s, soft-spoken and never given to throwing his weight around. Working with

Harry Miller had given him a background any engineer might envy, and like Miller he was accessible to the lowest-paid mechanic, yet wasn't impressed by the most officious vice president.

Deliberate in action and speech, Offutt seemed out of place in his office, where his men worked with him, rather than under him. He wore a hearing aid which, in the office, was usually turned off because he couldn't tune out the electric typewriters. At heart he was a monkey wrench engineer. He could solve his problems on paper and did, but when the job was being put together Offutt usually was there ready to take a hand, and see that it was done right.

Another Indianapolis veteran was Gene Haustein, who worked with Tucker and was an all-around test driver, mechanic and trouble shooter. Haustein knew automobiles from the grease rack to the track. Like Offutt he was soft-spoken and direct, unimpressed by titles or rank, and ready to take on any job that needed to be done. One day there was a press conference when a demonstration car was needed fast, and Tucker was nowhere in sight. Haustein was the only man in the place who would take a car out of the line without waiting to get permission from somebody. He drove it up, brought it to a smooth stop, and took newsmen for one of the most thrilling demonstrations in their experience.

But men like Offutt and Haustein and Leabu didn't impress the bankers, who wanted titles, even if the titles by now were meaningless. Offutt and the men with him got the job done and effectively, but they didn't have the prestige to attract heavy money.

While Tucker lost some good people through the resignations, he was picking up others as he went along and, for the time at least, was breaking about even. One of the most impressive in the new crop of VIPs was Philip Lockner, who rattled diamonds in his hands the way other people jingle small change or keys. Lockner always seemed to be as well supplied with money as with diamonds, and was rumored to have a diamond mine in his basement. His association with Tucker started in the rain early one Monday morning in New York.

Max Garavito arrived at his office at 39 Pearl Street about 9 o'clock and found a man huddled against the side of the building. He unlocked the door and took the man into his office, which extended across the block with another entrance on Church Street. Then he heard somebody beating on the Church Street door. The man at the other door was Lockner.

The two men had raced all the way from Cape Town, South Africa, to get a Tucker franchise, and had missed each other by minutes at various stops along the route. The race ended in a tie when they took off their coats in Garavito's office. Before they even sat down both men were talking at once. Garavito interrupted, suggesting that they go out and talk it over at breakfast.

When they got back they had agreed that Lockner would take the distributorship and split the dealerships with the other man, whose name is lost somewhere in the dusty records. South Africa was taken care of.

Lockner paid $80,000 for his franchise and became the corporation's biggest stockholder with 50,000 shares, which cost him $250,000. As was fitting for the biggest stockholder, Tucker had him elected a vice president and director. (For another $250,000 Tucker probably would have resigned and had him appointed president.) Lockner spent a lot of time at the plant and had a part in making some important decisions, but none of them saved his investment. When he finally gave up he stopped in New York to dump his stock, causing a serious but temporary slump in the price.

Throughout the next six months the Tucker plant looked like an annex of the United Nations, with people of almost every nationality and color passing through. Movie stars, generals, pugilists, visiting royalty and foreign capitalists rubbed shoulders in Tucker's reception room, and broke bread with the peasants in the plant cafeteria.

Between greeting important visitors, discussing deals and holding up his end of intramural arguments, Tucker had little time for his engineering department, which was beginning to despair of ever getting the Tin Goose to a point of production. Tucker wasn't overly concerned. He felt completely confident that a satisfactory design would be worked out.

But he was worried about the shortage of body steel at the time, and still more worried about digging up new sources of capital before they got in another bind. Even with the $17,000,000 in the bank, he knew there would be rough times ahead before income reached the break-even point.

18

Steel, Politics and Piston Liners

MANY PEOPLE AT THE PLANT THOUGHT TUCKER WAS CRAZY, trying to get his own source for steel before production lines were even set up. Some thought he had delusions of grandeur, trying to build an empire on what was still a shoestring, compared with the capital and resources of even the smallest independent.

But he wasn't as crazy as many believed and he wasn't entirely visionary. His efforts to get his own steel plant, like his purchase of Aircooled Motors, were not only to insure a controlled source of supply, but also to strengthen the company with separate sources of income.

The first try for steel failed, even though Tucker was high bidder, with his offer of $2,751,000 well over the "fair value" of $2,500,000 set for the plant by War Assets. The plant was a government-owned blast furnace at Granite City, Illinois, operated by Koppers Company, Inc., under lease. Bidders were Tucker, the Fulton Iron Company of Cleveland and a new company, Missouri-Illinois Furnaces of Granite City, or-

129

ganized only the week before with half its stock owned by Koppers.

All the bids were rejected, but with the rejection WAA announced that the plant had been sold to the new company fronting for Koppers for $3,255,000. What happened was that WAA boosted "fair value" of the plant without notice either to Tucker or Fulton Iron, which automatically disqualified their bids, and sold the plant to the Koppers firm for $5,000 over the new fair value figure.

Petition for an injunction to prevent sale of the plant to Koppers interests was dismissed by the U.S. Court of Appeals, on grounds that the government, in the person of WAA, had not consented to be sued. Associate Justice Bennett Champ Clark, who wrote the opinion, said:

"The transactions in the case are surrounded by a pervasive and most offensive odor of skulduggery. It is perfectly evident to anyone who takes the trouble to examine the record that the adjusting of the 'fair value' by the appellee (WAA) could only result in insuring that the Koppers interests secured this property."

Undaunted, Tucker was ready with another bid when WAA announced that a blast furnace and coke plant at Cleveland would be disposed of "as early as possible" through negotiations. If he missed here Tucker would be out in the cold, because it was the last government-owned steel plant.

Again Tucker was high bidder, over Republic Steel. He had the money, too, but again both bids were rejected, this time as "inadequate." When Tucker tried to find out how he could become adequate WAA slipped in a new hooker: he would have to come up with proof that he could get all the materials he needed, not only to operate the steel plant but to build automobiles as well.

This was a far bigger deal than the one in Granite City, rated the world's largest blast furnace and reportedly earning as high as a million dollars a month. Tucker almost knocked himself out getting options on ore, coal and limestone, and firm commitments on lake boats to haul the ore. Altogether he estimated they spent close to a quarter of a million dollars, not including $100,000 "earnest money" tendered with the first bid.

130

During negotiations a group of big wheels from WAA came to the Chicago plant to check progress, and minor employes melted into the background as the WAA men stalked through the plant and offices with grim faces, a small but impressive parade headed by Jess Larson, administrator. Actually they were just a bunch of guys working for the government in Washington, but to Tucker people they personified the Last Judgment.

And about this time Senator Ferguson jumped down Tucker's throat again with a new investigation, charging WAA with "gross mismanagement" in its disposal of war properties, including certain dealings with Kaiser-Frazer. Charges against K-F were innocuous and the company brushed them off casually. Tucker was Ferguson's real target, and in the end he was the one who was really hurt. Within three months after Ferguson's new attack started, and nine months after the beginning of negotiations, the plant was leased to Kaiser, with an option to buy, for less than either Tucker or Republic had offered. Tucker's only printable comment was that "War Assets must have got itself confused with the maternity and child welfare departments.

The search for an engine, and the resulting purchase of Aircooled Motors, was more successful. Even before the fight for steel was well under way, Tucker and his board had agreed on at least one point: that the "589" engine still needed too much development work for an automobile that had to be ready within months. The same was true of the double torque converters. Even if they could be worked out, there wasn't time to wait for them now.

There were several possibilities. The Jacobs Aircraft Engine Company at Pottstown, Pennsylvania, had advertised a liquid-cooled six-cylinder opposed light aircraft engine that looked pretty close to what Tucker wanted. But on investigation he found that the engine wasn't even in production, and to develop a design Tucker could use he would almost have to start over. A $100,000 development contract with Jacobs was canceled after innumerable delays, as was a similar contract with the Hoffman Motor Development Company at Detroit.

When efforts to get an engine developed outside failed, Tucker stepped in and set up his own program, and if the

131

board didn't want to approve they could resign. He sent his own men to his Ypsilanti plant where they were put on the payroll, and gave his own shop a contract to develop an engine. There, he said, they could work without interference and red tape, away from the endless bickering and controversy which had developed in Chicago. In Ypsilanti they could buy what they needed without waiting days or weeks for approval and purchase orders.

Heading the project were Eddie Offutt, then in the experimental department in Chicago, and Dan Leabu, who had been working with Offutt. With them went Tucker's oldest son, Preston, Jr., who had left an engineering course at the University of Michigan to work with his father.

"Press called Eddie and me, and said you guys come back with an engine in three months or we fold up," Leabu said.

Offutt took the men he wanted from Chicago. They hired two draftsmen in Ypsilanti and another from Detroit, and started to work in the big building behind Tucker's house. Offutt and Leabu were transferred to the Ypsilanti payroll January 12, and they delivered the first engine to Chicago March 6, just fifty-five days later.

G. A. (Andy) Anderson, Tucker's pilot on the Beechcraft, had been urging him to investigate the Franklin engine, which he said was one of the best and most reliable power plants in use on smaller aircraft. Tucker had been thinking along the same lines, so when the Ypsilanti project started they bought four Franklin six-cylinder opposed air-cooled engines from the Bell Aircraft Corporation at Niagara Falls, where they put the engines in helicopters for agricultural use.

All Offutt's crew had to work with were the engines and assembly drawings, which didn't include dimensions. So they took an engine completely apart and measured it, working with micrometers, surface plates and height gauges. When they had their own detailed drawings, Offutt started redesigning the engine to meet specifications he and Tucker had agreed on: an aluminum crank-case, blocks and heads; water cooling; 7:1 compression ratio; better than 150 horsepower and cruising speed at 1750 revolutions per minute, around 80 to 90 miles an hour. The original engine was 335 cubic inches, rated at approximately 178 horsepower at 3000 rpm. At 4250 rpm it should have delivered around 300 horsepower, comparable to present engines.

They had to change the blocks and heads for liquid cooling, add a flywheel and bell housing for attaching the transmission, and add an oil pan, since in the helicopter the engine operated in a vertical position.

The men worked in shifts, often around the clock. As fast as Offutt approved various parts, the prints were rushed to pattern shops, and as soon as patterns were ready they went directly to foundries for castings. The first manifolds were cut and welded from heavy sheet iron by Herman Ringling, who had shaped the body of the Tin Goose. Some machining was done in the shop about a block away, which was still equipped for production and tool work. Jobs that could be done faster outside were farmed out.

Part by part they went through the entire engine, and about the only features that remained of the original Franklin were the dimensions, the crank-case, crank-shaft, connecting rods and pistons. Tucker wanted to use as many of the original parts as possible, but comparatively few were adapted to the new design.

Converting to liquid cooling called for addition of a water pump, and the camshaft was changed for better idling, which wasn't important in aircraft. Some of the timing gears were replaced with fiber to reduce noise. A standard automobile generator and starter were added, and by the time they got through it wasn't a Franklin engine any more. But it was still an engine whose performance had been proved with countless thousands of hours of flying time under almost any weather conditions that could be imagined.

Before the first casting for the blocks had cooled off Leabu hauled them from the foundry in a pickup and set them in a jig mill, and when they were ready he brought them back to put in cylinder liners. They already had the liners, a standard size of alloyed steel from Thompson Products. After weeks of hard, almost continuous work the end of the job was in sight, and they decided not to stop until they finished it.

They turned Mrs. Tucker's kitchen into a heat treat department with Mrs. Tucker furnishing the oven, though she didn't know it at the time. They set up a progressive assembly line starting on the back steps, and popped the first two blocks

133

into the oven of the electric stove. It took about three hours to get them up to between 500 and 600 degrees, which was as high as the oven would go. As soon as they were heated through they were set on burners on top of the stove to keep them hot, and two more blocks were stuck in the oven and the blocks outside moved up a step.

Equipment for installing the liners was all ready and consisted chiefly of two large cans, of the kind fruit comes in for restaurants. The larger of the two cans was set on the floor and the smaller one placed inside of it. Then the sleeves were placed one at a time in the smaller inside can, covered with naptha to keep them from frosting so they would slide into the blocks easily. To cool them, liquid oxygen was poured into the space between the cans from a thermos-like jug.

One at a time the blocks were set on the kitchen floor on bricks, to keep them level and not burn holes in the linoleum. Then one of the men, wearing asbestos gloves, took a liner and slid it into the cylinder opening in the block. Heat had expanded the hole in the block and cold contracted the liner, but it had to be put in fast before it started to expand again.

While the liner expanded it made a shrill humming sound until it was locked in place, and if it went in crooked the only way to get it out was to break it with a hammer, knock out the pieces and start over. On the first block they only lost one liner.

Within eleven hours after the first blocks were put in the oven, the first engine was together and ready for test. In a garage space in the front of the building the engine was set on a makeshift stand, with a garden hose connected to the water inlet on the block and a five-gallon can of gasoline hung overhead, connected to the carburetor with a length of rubber tubing. A flexible tube running under the garage door carried off the exhaust. It was still winter in Ypsilanti.

After a few moments the engine took off. It was a climax, but everybody was too tired to celebrate. They let it run about five minutes, yanked off the gasoline and water connections and the flexible exhaust tube, and threw the engine in the back of a pickup. Offutt and Leabu took off for Chicago, and Tucker had an engine—and with the engine were patterns and temporary tooling for making at least another hundred.

* * *

The only one who lost in the whole deal was Mrs. Tucker, whose stove was ruined. Where they had set the blocks on the top burners, the whole top of the stove sagged in the middle. Preston Junior thought it was only fair that his mother get a new stove out of it, so he added the price to the bill which went to the board of directors for approval. One of them took a second look.

"What the hell kind of a business are we in?" he demanded.

Preston Junior explained what had happened. The board approved the item unanimously, but Tucker wouldn't let it go through.

"If this gets out people aren't going to understand," he said. "The auditors are going to make an issue of it and before we're through some stockholder will be yelling his head off. I'll buy the damn stove myself."

On March 21 Tucker announced the purchase of Aircooled Motors, which built the Franklin engine, from Republic Aviation Corporation for $1,800,000. He had accomplished a double purpose, the same which had motivated him in going after the steel plants: he had a controlled source of supply and a separate source of income for the corporation.

Tucker faced a lot of bitter opposition inside the corporation when he bought Aircooled and was criticized severely outside, but the years since have vindicated his judgment. Aircooled Motors has made an average net profit of half a million dollars a year after taxes, and the plant's present minimum value is estimated at $3,500,000.

With preliminary design and temporary tooling complete, Offutt and his men went back to Ypsilanti and finished three more engines, and after the corporation bought Aircooled, further refinement and testing were transferred there.

The bill to Tucker Corporation for the job was $114,215, which was comparable to the amounts asked for development by other companies. But there was a difference, more important than the price. This time they got an engine—not one engine but four, with patterns and tooling—and they got it fast, in less than two months.

No one ever claimed the engine was perfect for the automobile. Work was being done constantly to improve its performance. Engines in some of the cars were a bit temperamental but they performed, and there are people driving Tuckers today who will put the Tucker engine against new V-8's for all-around performance and reliability. Most of the troubles seemed to be in carburation and timing, and both could be solved long before cars were in quantity production.

When they first tested the new engine in Chicago it looked for a while as if Offutt and his crew had goofed. The engine was running hot and nobody could understand why, until one of the engineers from Aircooled took a closer look.

In the rush to test the engine before leaving Ypsilanti, somebody had put the fan on backwards.

136

19

A Homey
Stockholders' Meeting

THE APPROACHING FIRST ANNUAL STOCKHOLDERS' MEETING by no means presented a crisis, as things in general were going smoothly, but it did create a problem which would have solved itself with a little more time.

At least one car had to be ready to show the stockholders, one reasonable facsimile of the car being readied for production. The engine was no longer a problem, because the Aircooled plant had all the necessary equipment and technical experts to finish the job. But the transmission was still lacking.

Tucker had offered $5,000 cash for an automatic transmission that would be an improvement over Buick's Dynaflow, and comparable in performance to the Hydramatic. A young engineer, Warren A. Rice, soon claimed the reward and was paid the $5,000 as soon as Tucker was satisfied that his design would work.

While waiting for a working model, which promised to take some time, they decided on a four-speed manual shift to bridge the gap until they had time to shake all the bugs out of the automatic. Efforts to have a manual job developed outside had ended about the same way as the engine—a contract with one company was canceled, and all the proposals reached astronomical figures, with delivery dates months ahead.

Tucker didn't have months to spare, so he followed his new policy of making decisions himself. Again he drafted Offutt and Leabu and sent them to his Ypsilanti plant, which was given a contract to develop the manual job.

Offutt went to work immediately on the design and Leabu went scouring the country for Cord transmissions, to be adapted for the Tucker until the Y-1 ("Y" standing for Ypsilanti) was ready. They chose Cord because it had front drive, with the engine placed backwards as in the Tucker.

Leabu scavenged junk yards and used car lots from Detroit to Miami and finally rounded up (anonymously) twenty-two Cord transmissions. Some were good and others had a few usable parts. Altogether eighteen were installed in Tucker cars to get them on the road, and as the new Y-1's were finished, all but four had the Cord transmissions removed and the Y-1's put in.

For the new manual job they designed a pre-selector electric-type shift; a short lever on the steering column selected the gear, and the transmission shifted when the clutch was depressed. Actual shifting was done by vacuum, somewhat similar to Chevrolet in the late 40s, but with the valves actuated by electromagnets.

SEC's experts later reported triumphantly that the Cord transmission "through later tests proved to be utterly inadequate." This was no secret to Tucker or the men working on it. They knew it was too light for the more powerful Tucker engine before making the first installation, but it would serve the immediate purpose, and Tucker knew that the new automatic would perform with anything on the road.

The Y-1 project went pretty much like the engine, but took longer because of the difficulty of getting gears cut to order. Leabu said except for a few bolts, washers and miscellaneous items, no parts in the Cord were interchangeable with the Y-1, including the electric-and-vacuum control assemblies. It was a completely new transmission.

The Y-1 wasn't entirely satisfactory. Some said the gear angle was wrong and others said the gears were cut from soft iron. Most of this work was done in Detroit, where there were persistent reports that Tucker jobs were being sabotaged. Whatever the reason, it wasn't overly important, because all the Y-1's were due to be replaced later by the automatic. The whole job took less than three months, and a demonstrator was ready for the stockholders well ahead of time.

As reported by the Chicago papers, the meeting was a gala event. Tucker himself drove the car in a demonstration run, receiving wild applause when he showed it could back up. Many in the audience had been worrying about this privately, and had come for the sole purpose of finding out for themselves if the reports were true.

The *Chicago Daily News,* under the head, TUCKER CO. HAS HOMEY STOCKHOLDERS' MEETING, said nearly 1,700 turned out in the big meeting hall at the Tucker plant. "They streamed down the corridors, men and women with children, some bobby-soxers, city firemen in uniform, a very large mass of humanity in a single place," the *News* reported.

"This demonstration," reported the *Chicago Tribune,* "was the climax of one of the most unusual stockholder meetings in Chicago history. The large number of shareholders, assembled in a room bedecked with flags and bunting and entertained with musical recordings, asked not a single question about production, dividends, or other corporate matters. The harmonious group, whose meeting was opened with a prayer, were told only that cars were coming in the not too distant future."

With the stockholders out of his hair for another year, Tucker concentrated on getting the new automatic transmission into production. A test model of the R-1 (the "R" standing for Rice) was built in the shop at the plant and installed in a chassis; others were installed later in some of the cars. From the first there was no possible doubt about its performance. Inside the plant grounds a car with a Rice transmission was placed beside a Buick Dynaflow in loose rock.

Mechanics said the Tucker walked out easily, while the Buick stalled and refused to move.

The reason was simple. In most automatic transmissions of the time there was a period, while the car started to get under motion, in which the fluid coupling or torque converter had to reach a certain speed before it "took hold." This could be felt as a sort of whirring sensation, while speed of the engine was still above the car's speed.

In the Rice design the transmission was in positive gear as soon as the engine got above idling speed, and it started pulling immediately. It was demonstrated that the car would push-start at ten miles an hour, while a speed of twenty or higher was needed for other automatic jobs. A favorite story at the time concerned a man who was stalled and a woman who offered to give him a push.

"This is an automatic transmission," the man said, "and you'll have to get up to thirty-five miles an hour to get me started."

While the man waited he happened to glance up at his rear-view mirror. He saw the woman barreling down the road toward his car. She was going 35 miles an hour.

As soon as the first automatic transmission was installed and tested in a chassis, Tucker took it and two other cars to Detroit to challenge the enemy on his home grounds. Police permission was obtained to hold the demonstration in Rouge Park on Detroit's west side, and the cars were left overnight in a lot to be ready for the next day. Early the following morning there was a minor traffic jam at Evergreen and Joy Road as hundreds of drivers stopped to look at the Tuckers, peer under them, shake the bodies up and down and kick the tires.

Detroit automotive writers are a skeptical lot, but enthusiasm for the new transmission was unanimous. Leo Donovan, writing in his automotive column in the *Detroit Free Press*, was thrilled.

"Remember your first ride in a roller-coaster?" he wrote. "The slow ascent, the gradual turn high in the air—then the awful plunge into space?

"We had our first ride in the rear-engine Tucker Torpedo

in Rouge Park Wednesday. The sensation was not unlike that first roller-coaster ride.

"The Tucker Torpedo demonstration on Spinoza Drive was conducted on an open chassis driven by Warren Rice, a Tucker Corp. engineer who is directing the Chicago company's transmission development program.

"We went up a 7 percent grade, creeping. Rice made a slow U-turn and then stepped on the accelerator.

"We plunged down the dinky incline so fast it seemed the grade was twice as sharp. The speedometer fluctuated between 60 and 70 miles an hour.

"Later, from a standing start, the chassis achieved about 60 miles an hour by the speedometer in about 10 seconds.

"At a luncheon meet preceding the demonstration, Rice sought to explain the technical operation of the new automatic transmission. A few heads nodded knowingly at his references, but representatives of the press confided still later that his explanation was only a confusion.

"But the transmission worked. And good."

In the *Detroit Times,* Siler Freeman said the transmission is something "that may be revolutionary, if it can be made on the production line. It gives a quick surge of power smoothly and accelerates at a terrific pace, we noted riding up front with Warren Rice, who helped develop it."

Ralph R. Watts of the *Detroit News* was more impressed with learning that the car would go backwards at close to 50 miles an hour. Due to a peculiarity of design the transmission would drive the car much faster than standard transmissions in reverse; it wasn't planned that way and was no particular advantage.

There were only three positions on the selector dial: drive, neutral and reverse. Rice explained that the design provided all the torque needed under all conditions without the additional "low" position for emergency power which other missions had. In other words there was no need for a "low" because the engine started pulling immediately in low gear.

There also was no heat exchanger, or separate provision for cooling oil in the fluid couplings, because they didn't heat up. At 100 miles an hour the tachometer showed 3300 rpm, compared to 5100 and 5300 for two other stock cars of the same year. There was no clutch, only the brake and accelerator pedals on the floor.

It was strictly the truth when Tucker told the press conference that the transmission had only twenty-eight basic moving parts, compared to hundreds of parts in comparable automatic designs. It had a no-creep provision, which is still a problem in some transmissions, and would have been far cheaper to manufacture in production than any other design then in use.

While Tucker ultimately lost the war, he won the transmission battle hands down, and in planning entire production with automatic transmissions, he showed vision that has since been vindicated.

The spring of 1948 had been reasonably calm by Tucker standards, with no more than the normal number of crises, which meant one every few weeks. For Tucker, the greatest personal loss was the death of Jimmy Sakuyama.

Jimmy had come to Chicago and was living in his trailer inside the plant area, near the hospital where he could get quick attention when he fell sick. He still worked almost every day at his drawing board in the engineering department, wearing two pairs of thick glasses one over the other and drawing lines so fine they might have been etched. But he could no longer put in 24 to 36 hours without stopping, as he used to do in New Orleans and Ypsilanti when there was some job that couldn't wait. Even his bouts with the bottle were far between, and seemed to be more for carrying on a tradition than any actual need. Jimmy was sick.

During his last illness he had given Tucker a name and address in Japan and asked him to send word there after his death. Tucker sent the cable and received an immediate reply: someone would come for the ashes. Jimmy had asked to be cremated. At the funeral there were only Tucker and his wife, Tucker's mother and two other friends, Gene Haustein, who had known Jimmy in New Orleans and Ypsilanti, and Harold Tellock, in the engineering department, who met him first in Chicago and respected his ability.

Two days after Tucker sent the cable two Japanese men

came to the plant. People in the office said they looked like twins, dressed exactly alike in black suits, black shoes, and black hats. One of them carried a green vase about eighteen inches high with a matching cover. They thought it was jade, probably a funeral urn.

Jimmy had said many times he had disgraced his noble family and would never return. But in death Jimmy went back to Japan, to join his honorable ancestors.

20

One for the Road

LONG AGO IT USED TO BE SAID THAT LOVE MAKES THE WORLD go 'round. Maybe today it's nuclear fission. But in 1949 it was money, and that was Tucker's problem when design of the automobile was far enough along to start getting first models to dealers.

A pilot assembly line had been set up and engines and body panels were being delivered, but they had to finish paying for dies and tooling, and buy materials to start production. The stock issue had fallen $5,000,000 short of its goal, and the tussles to get the stock cleared and trying for a steel plant had cost heavily in time and money.

A long-range program for outside income had already been set up with hiring of Secundo Campini, who became the newest vice president. Campini, along with Frank Whittle of England, was one of the pioneers in the new field of jet propulsion, and was credited with the first jet-powered flight from Milan to Rome in August of 1940, in a Campini-Caproni plane. (Authorities differ, some giving credit for the first flight to a German in 1939. If Campini was second, he was

144

The man and the car.

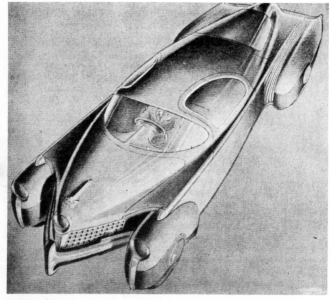

One of the first artist's conceptions of the Tucker "Torpedo" showed the driver's seat in the center, a rear-engine compartment, a "Cyclops Eye" center light, and doors opening into the roof.

Tucker's first design had a center driver's seat slightly ahead of seats on either side. The side seats swiveled, as illustrated, for easy entrance. Later, Tucker decided on a conventional front seat for first models.

Grinning engineers and mechanics hoist Tucker to their shoulders after working all night getting the Tin Goose ready for its World Premiere. Nobody knows how the name "Tin Goose" originated, but it was used affectionately by the men working on the car.

Tucker and his wife stand by as daughter Marilyn, 20, clobbers the famous Tin Goose with a bottle of champagne at the World Premiere. Preparations were made for three thousand people, but more than five thousand showed up.

Roy S. Durstine, left, head of the Durstine advertising agency in New York, and Floyd D. Cerf, who handled the $15,000,000 stock issue; and Tucker. These two men helped put Tucker in business.

Eddie Offutt holds the left end of the windshield that popped out, as advertised, when the car rolled over during a test run on the Indianapolis Speedway. Offutt had only a slight bruise—the car was driven away after a tire was changed.

Side view of the Tucker '48 with Preston Tucker at the wheel.

still ahead of the first flight made in England, using Whittle's engine.)

Campini was brought in by Enea Bossi, who had worked with Tucker in New Orleans and went to Europe to see what he could find in automobile development that Tucker could use. While in Italy he met Campini, a former acquaintance, and recommended him to Tucker.

Tucker's immediate purpose was to get work for the plant from the Air Force, which was interested in the Italian engineer from the start. Second, he wanted to start Campini on development of a gasoline turbine for future use in the automobile. Tucker met some opposition hiring Campini, but he told the board it would be a long time before they made any profits from automobiles, and even then they would need diversification.

"If you think we're going to make automobiles alone you're crazy," he told a board meeting. "We'll make a lot of things. Any independent that isn't diversified will never make the grade, no matter how good an automobile it produces."

Whether Campini was the genius Tucker believed him to be may have been debatable, but the Army was interested enough that it offered to fly him from Italy in a military plane, Campini said later. Campini set up his own department in the plant and started shuttling back and forth from Wright-Patterson field at Dayton, where there was every promise that the company would get a development contract from the Air Force.

But that did not solve any immediate problems, and Tucker knew it might be a long time before even the best of Campini's ideas could start paying off. It was the need for immediate money that inspired the Accessories Program, which was born of desperation and succeeded far beyond the wildest dreams.

The accessories plan was the brainchild of Cliff Knoble, advertising manager, whose idea was to sell accessories to people who wanted to buy Tucker automobiles, and with the accessories give them a sequence number for getting a car as soon as one with their number came off the line. The idea was a natural for the time, when it was practically impossible to buy a car that wasn't already loaded down with accessories; the chief difference was that Tucker buyers got the accessories first. While the plan was publicized as a means of beating the black market, the big objective was money. If successful, it had possibilities of raising at least part of the needed millions in months, or even weeks. The press release announcing the program said:

"In the Tucker control plan, buyers are offered now, for immediate delivery if desired, a desirable group of advance accessories including a radio, a set of fitted and immediately usable luggage, and tailored seat covers.

"With this advance purchase, the buyer receives written assurance by his dealer that he may buy for his own use, and no re-sale, a Tucker car in the same controlled sequence as he purchased the "Group A" package, as and when Tucker cars are received for delivery by the dealer."

A "kickoff" meeting was held May 17 at the Congress Hotel in Chicago, after which teams fanned out across the country. There was no problem of transportation because now the cars could be driven anywhere. On the Eastern swing most of the cars were driven and they made New York, Philadelphia, Washington, Boston, Cleveland, Pittsburgh, Columbus and other cities. The Western circuit involved longer jumps, so the Conestoga also was used, and the whirlwind tour included Minneapolis, Kansas City, Seattle, Oakland, San Francisco and Los Angeles.

In Washington a bus driver spotted a Tucker at the 16th Street entrance to the Statler Hotel. He immediately stopped his bus and went over for a closer look. Most of his passengers followed. Also in Washington, Tucker took some newspapermen for a ride, and when he turned into an alley beside a bank to turn around, a man rushed out of the bank yelling:

"It's true! It's true!"

The banker had just told him there wasn't any Tucker automobile.

146

If there were any questions about holding the audience, returns from the first broadcast answered them. More than 15,000 entries were received, said to be more than twice the response on other new contest programs. One letter ended:

"Sincerity, honesty and a desire to give rather than get should bring fruit. My best wishes go forward to send you Godspeed toward success in your work."

21

Look—No Hands!

WITH MONEY COMING IN FROM THE ACCESSORIES PROGRAM IT looked like good odds for starting at least limited production, and with a few hundred cars on the road the company should have smooth sailing. Body stampings were coming in from the Hayes Body Company in Grand Rapids, and permanent metal dies were expected by the end of July. Glenn Madden, purchasing agent, said the company had spent well over $4,000,000 on tooling.

"We are on the threshold of mass production," Madden said, "within ten months from the time we received the major part of our working capital. Even an established firm will normally take from eighteen months to two years to design and build an entirely new car, and it has been customary in the industry to spend at least a year changing a single model."

By comparison, Madden said one producer spent $37,000,000 retooling one model, almost twice what Tucker had to develop an entire automobile. *Automotive Industries* quoted Nash as saying their changeover would cost approximately $15,000,000, and reported Chrysler would spend about $75,000,000 on their new models. According to figures from the industry itself, Tucker's overall expenditure was low.

When the accessories program first came up for discussion I thought it was risky in that it could bring bad reaction unless deliveries of cars began within the next few months. Rockelman said they didn't have any choice, that they had to have money or go under, and this was a way to get it.

Rockelman was right about the plan raising money, because before it ended they collected more than $2,000,000. But I was right about the risk. This was the opening SEC had been waiting for to holler "Fraud!"

The plan was at least unusual, and fantastic in that it worked, but there was neither fraud nor misrepresentation. For every order taken accessories were delivered, or stored in the factory or by dealers. And buyers were told, and this was emphasized by dealers, that the automobile was still on a strictly if-as-and-when basis.

When the combined attack by SEC and the Justice Department started May 28, 1948, the first round with SEC appeared to be little more than a continuation of the sniping which had been going on since before the stock was registered. Tucker didn't realize at first how serious it was, partly because to some extent it was overshadowed by the death of Ralph Hepburn.

Hepburn had been racing since 1924, and only one driver had made more appearances in the famous "500." When he joined Tucker as Western zone manager in 1947 he stayed out of the race, but in 1948 he was determined to make one last try for the win he had so narrowly missed so many times. Nobody, including Tucker, could talk him out of it.

"I've got a lot of money tied up in you," Tucker told him, "and besides you can't stand to be broken up very many more times."

Hepburn was then 53 years old and walked with a marked limp, from earlier racing accidents.

"If I get hit this time I won't feel it," he said.

Hepburn was right. In a practice run May 18 he wound the big Novi up to 132 miles an hour, then skidded off into the infield in the northeast turn, swerved back across the track and into the concrete retaining wall, and was killed instantly. Tucker had made a special trip to Indianapolis for a last effort to persuade Hepburn not to drive. He was walking over to the track when he heard the crash.

When Tucker got back from the funeral at Glendale, California, he found plenty of problems to take his mind off Hepburn, the most serious of which was the new investigation. It opened officially May 28, but Tucker first heard about it after a meeting June 3 in the Chicago SEC offices, attended by James D. Coolidge, company attorney. There Coolidge was given a copy of the order for the investigation, and told it would be kept secret if the books and records were turned over voluntarily.

Coolidge said he would have to take it up with the company and would let them know as soon as possible. Next day he called James P. Goode of SEC and told him Tucker wanted to take the matter up with the board of directors, and the earliest it was possible to have a meeting was June 8.

Goode said he would clear with Washington, and called back later to tell Coolidge that Washington had authorized waiting until the following Tuesday, June 8.

On June 6, a Sunday night broadcast by Drew Pearson told of the new SEC investigation, and predicted a Department of Justice investigation that "would blow the new Chicago auto firm higher than a kite." When the information was leaked to Pearson it destroyed the last chance of keeping the investigation secret, as promised by SEC, whether Tucker cooperated or not. By this time Tucker was more than a little weary of such attacks because there was no way they could be answered.

To Tucker it was either a desire to destroy the corporation, or belated retaliation for his treatment of Ted Granik the year before, that prompted Pearson to make such an announcement over the air. Tucker had no possible knowledge how Pearson got the information, if indeed it were genuine, but ultimately it had to come from SEC.

Whatever the immediate source, it was a deadly blow. It was the kind of story that would have far-reaching effects, for simply to mention the Department of Justice was to throw suspicion on Tucker and the corporation, to make him appear guilty before any shred of evidence was produced. It created the kind of talk that Tucker in those days was continually fighting. As soon as one rumor was disproved, another appeared. Some men might have given up then. It only made Tucker more determined.

The rumor of a new investigation with a mention of the Justice Department brought immediate and disastrous results:

Tucker stock dropped to less than $3 a share, a loss of some $6,000,000 to stockholders.

The Air Force lost all interest in Campini.

The accessories program slowed almost to a standstill.

Creditors started pressing for their money.

Suppliers, who had been delivering parts and materials on the usual credit terms, suddenly demanded cash.

Dealers everywhere started worrying about their notes.

To make the situation still rougher, SEC demanded that the corporation's records be delivered to its regional office in Chicago. Tucker was stunned when he heard the Pearson broadcast, and he shook with rage when he learned that the news had leaked to Pearson before he even had a chance to comply. He refused to surrender the records, and SEC filed suit in Federal court.

"SEC made a pre-emptory demand for literally thousands of our files and records," Tucker said in a press release. "Tying up our records at this time will make it impossible to continue operating."

Thomas B. Hart, SEC regional administrator, said Tucker was confusing the issue, that SEC had no intention of interfering with production of cars. In the court hearing Tucker surrendered, and said SEC could investigate his records in the plant. At the same time he laid off close to 1,600 employees and said the plant would be closed until the investigation was over.

He had to close. Trying to work with SEC men swarming over the offices would have shattered the morale of employees, and scared the wits out of dealers and distributors visiting the plant. While it wasn't entirely true that the company couldn't operate with SEC checking its records, it was true that Tucker couldn't raise a dime of outside money while the investigation was going full force, with continuous reports that the FBI was on his trail for fraud.

153

About quitting time one afternoon, when things looked blackest, a few executives assembled in Tucker's office to try to figure some way out of the mess. Somebody suggested that a drink might help. A secretary knocked on the door and much to her surprise was handed a glass and invited to stay. Some of the office help drifted in, and as the word got around they were joined by men from the shop, still in greasy work clothes. Everybody had a few drinks and some, including Tucker, got a bit high.

Some of us in publicity feared that Tucker might lose the respect of his few remaining employees, but we were wrong. The effect was exactly the opposite. Their reaction seemed to be one of pleased surprise and approval, in effect:

"He's human, just like we are. He's got worries and problems, just like we have."

Tucker had never had his employees so solidly behind him.

Even Tucker officials didn't realize how far SEC intended to go until they received a six-page letter listing the records they wanted. The list covered five pages, single spaced, and included the corporation's entire activities since April of 1947: books, correspondence, minutes of board meetings, contracts—in short, everything.

They even demanded all the engineering reports, a mass of material that SEC's few technical men couldn't have evaluated in a year and the rest couldn't even have understood, much less analyzed. In addition to files from the Chicago plant SEC wanted records—presumably down to the last memorandum from two Tucker subsidiaries, the export office in New York and the Canadian branch in Toronto. With Air-cooled Motors in Syracuse now a wholly owned subsidiary, its records would likewise be subject to Hart's demands.

To Tucker, the real reason for WAA's rejection of his bid for the Cleveland steel plant was Ferguson's outburst a week earlier, and he also believed that enemies in the auto industry in Detroit had pulled wires to provoke this new investigation.

"It didn't just happen," he told associates, "that War Assets threw out our bid the same day this new investigation started. Whoever's back of it is sure as hell covering all the angles, because War Assets knows we've got the money, they know we need the plant to stay in business over the long haul,

154

"Gee, you got a swell boss," the motor cop told employees riding on the float behind.

The procession started sedately enough, but before long it developed into what one reporter called "one of the dizziest motor parades in the memory of local traffic cops." Heading south, the first fifty or so cars went so fast they lost the rest by about five minutes, and when the rest tried to catch up a tail section broke off.

By the time the cars and floats had turned around at 22nd Street, three separate parades were heading north towards the Loop, and when the last two sections tried short cuts to catch up, the result was one of the finest traffic jams in the city's history. At Wacker Drive and Dearborn Street they came in from three directions, with impatient motorists horning in between.

When the paraders got back to the plant, they agreed ruefully that there was little they could do, but at least Tucker knew they were on his side.

22

"This Car Is Really Dynamite!"

SHORTLY AFTER THE PARADE THE FIRST IN A SERIES OF suits was filed in Federal Court asking that a receiver be appointed, asserting the corporation was "in danger of financial collapse," and charging Tucker officials with mismanagement.

A few days earlier a stockholders' suit was filed by a New York dealer on the strength of 100 shares bought a few days before, Tucker attorneys said, for the sole purpose of filing the suit. These and succeeding suits set the theme for the charge, repeated across the country, that "no car of any kind, other than the experimental car, has been produced."

That this could be taken seriously by a court anywhere that newspapers existed seemed unbelievable. Tucker cars had been driven and displayed all over the country only a short time before during the accessories program. It was even more fantastic in Chicago, where the seven Tucker cars in the employees' parade made headlines in every newspaper in town.

Before the summons had been served in the receivership action Tucker called a closed meeting at the plant, attended by about 1,000 dealers. During the meeting a U.S. marshal arrived to serve the summons, and with him came an associate of the attorney who filed the action. This man tried to crash the gate. Tucker threw him out personally, flashing a deputy sheriff's badge he had acquired some time before during a political campaign.

Dealers were urged to pay on their notes so the company could continue operating; a few wrote out checks and others promised to send them in later. Two days later another suit was filed, charging Tucker with illegal arrest for tossing out the attorney, Julian C. Ryer.

While the plant was closed Phil S. Hanna, financial and automotive writer for the *Chicago Daily News*, went to see for himself what the situation actually looked like. He wanted to know whether Tucker was close to production as he claimed, or if he was just putting on a show as claimed by SEC.

"The first thing that strikes the eye," Hanna wrote, "is literally several acres of wheels, tires, body stampings, engines, frames and all the related parts that go to make up an automobile. You see hundreds of cylinder blocks, bell housings, radios, batteries and shock absorbers.

"I counted 58 finished car bodies in the assembly line. Work was stopped on these a week ago when the Securities and Exchange Commission moved in to investigate financing of the company.

"In another bay of the big factory close by I counted 90 finished engines.

"There are small mountains of cartons containing smaller parts for the automobile in the receiving room, a huge stack of sheet metal and a battery of shelves half a city block long containing steel bars and rods.

"In the forefront of the mammoth factory, on the Cicero Ave. side, conveyers and new welding machinery, part of the assembly line, appear ready to resume operations at a moment's notice.

"In another big room I saw about 30 Tucker workmen putting cars together and tuning them up. These men are

159

working 'for free,' and since the closing of the plant have assembled six cars.

"I talked with two of them, Eddie Offutt and Dan Leabu, who told me that they were working 'for free' because they have faith in Tucker and believe the SEC investigation will prove 'political.'

"One of the men took me out in a new Tucker which was just being completed. Then he took me out in a chassis equipped with Tucker's new automatic transmission.

"I had no stopwatch to check acceleration but from a standing start we got up to 60 miles an hour faster than I can recall having ridden before.

"The car backed up rapidly.

"Coming and going into the plant are scores of Tucker dealers from all over the United States. I heard no disgruntled conversation.

"I saw the offices which the SEC claimed to have cost $110,000. The walls are covered with imitation woodwork in wallpaper. Cost of remodeling was $10,600 and air conditioning $7,500, according to books shown me.

"The Tucker plant, according to what I saw, appears ready to start production of cars."

About three weeks after the plant was shut down for the investigation, Tucker had money from the accessories program and from partial payments by dealers on close to $5,000,000 in notes, held by the company as payment for franchises. The receivership suits were no longer making the front page, and seemed to be accepted as one of the hazards of being in business.

With some of the heat off, Tucker decided to start operating again even with SEC in the plant, hoping he could prove to the government that he could go ahead if they would just get off his back. So the latter part of July the plant reopened, recalling about 300 production workers, only a fraction of the force that had been working before the investigation started.

With enough money to pay for parts and materials on a piecemeal basis, they started putting more automobiles together. Neither Tucker nor any of the men working on the

160

cars ever pretended the production line would turn out 1,000 cars a day, or even 100, though production people in the plant said 100 a day could be run through with a big enough force. Tucker called it a "pilot production line," which it was. It would get enough cars built to shake out the bugs, and show what changes were needed when they were ready for a faster, bigger line.

The Securities & Exchange commission said it was a "mock production line." The difference seemed to be a matter of semantics.

Tucker believed that Thomas Hart, the SEC regional administrator, was motivated by some personal grudge, though he could never understand what it could have been. Tall, solemn and taciturn, Hart seldom smiled in public, and whenever Tucker was mentioned he seemed to stiffen with rage. Comparatively obscure as an official, Hart exercised tremendous power behind the scenes, and he was the moving, directing force behind SEC's continuous and unrelenting campaign against Tucker and the corporation. To Hart there seemed to be no gradations between right and wrong, and he pursued his methodical, painstaking investigations of Tucker with almost missionary zeal.

In August, while the SEC was working in the offices and a short force was trying to assemble cars in the factory, there came the first public recognition of the automobile by an acknowledged authority on cars. It was a story in the August issue of *Mechanix Illustrated* by Tom McCahill, who probably has a wider following among automobile fans than any other writer in the country. McCahill wrote:

"Tucker is building an automobile! And, brother, it's a *real* automobile! I want to go on record right here and now as saying that it is the most amazing American car I have ever seen to date; its performance is out of this world. Why do I think so? Wait until you have had an opportunity to drive the car and you'll know what I mean."

From coast to coast, McCahill wrote, he had talked with automobile men, and whenever the subject got around to Tucker, smiles and guffaws were always in order.

"I was told by men who said they had it right from the horse's mouth, that Tucker was in an engineering jam because he couldn't figure out a way to get a reverse gear into his car.

161

I was told by others that his only car had a Mercury engine under the hood.''

McCahill saw the factory where men were assembling cars, he saw the line of bodies, engines ready for installation, thousands of parts and piles of raw materials, with machines and production equipment ready to go. He was given a ride, and then he drove the car himself.

And McCahill was no novice. He has an earned reputation for panning anything he doesn't like in pungent and picturesque language, and he doesn't care whether a car sells for $1,000 or $10,000—if he doesn't like it, he says so. Of the Tucker's performance he wrote:

''The pre-select shift worked well and the car took off like a comet. After several acceleration runs I stopped and tried reverse gear. The Tucker does back up! Leaving the plant grounds, I went up to Cicero Boulevard on the south side of Chicago, and soon I knew I was in one of the *greatest performing passenger automobiles* ever built on this side of the Atlantic.

''This car is real dynamite! I accelerated from a dead standstill to 60 miles an hour in 10 seconds. Then I saw an open stretch ahead so I opened the throttle wide. In no time at all, it seemed, we were doing 90 on the clock, 95, 100 and then 105—miles an hour, that is! This was the quickest 105 miles an hour I have ever reached. I have gone 105 before in foreign cars but none of them ever got there that soon.

''The car is roomy and comfortable. It steers and handles better than any other American car I have driven. As to roadability, it's in a class by itself. I'll really go out on a limb and say that if this car will stand up and prove reliable, it will make every other car made in America look like Harrigan's hack with the wheels off. The car I was driving might start coming apart in 50 miles—that I don't know. But you have my word for it, when I was driving it, it was tops.''

If the SEC or anybody in the agency read McCahill's story they ignored it, because a constantly increasing force of SEC people plodded through records at the plant, day after day and week after week. The SEC force, which for a time outnumbered Tucker employees, finally left in September, after photostating thousands of records. Obviously the commission was in no hurry to finish its investigation, which continued more than a year longer.

To the government, every one of the Tuckers was a Tin Goose, and if all fifty had gone into orbit under their own power, SEC and the Justice Department wouldn't have admitted it, or probably even bothered to look out the window.

_23_

We Hit Every S.O.B. in the Country

WITH THE SQUEEZE FOR MONEY GETTING TIGHTER BY THE hour, as the government's leisurely investigation continued, Tucker decided to try again for private financing until the investigation cleared him. His best chance for success, he believed, was to prove beyond any possible doubt to the government, the public and possible financial angels that he had a product, and a good one.

To do this he sent seven Tuckers to Indianapolis, where Speedway officials gave him permission to use the track and barred the public during the tests. The two-and-one-half-mile oval was the toughest testing ground Tucker knew of, and he believed if the cars survived the tests they planned, even SEC might realize—and admit—that the Tucker car was a reality.

Eddie Offutt headed the test crew, and with him were some of Tucker's best men—Haustein, an experienced race driver; Leabu, whom Tucker had appointed general production manager a short time before; a crew of expert mechanics and drivers; and men from engineering to observe and report on mechanical performance.

Taking over some of the track service buildings, Offutt's men went to work with stop watches and charts to record speed, mileage, gas and oil consumption, engine temperature, tire wear and the many other factors which determine performance. Drivers reported on roadability, maneuverability, riding qualities, steering and general handling. The cars were there for two weeks, some of them driven continuously, twenty-four hours a day by drivers working in relays.

It was rather a grim experience riding around the track, going into turns at 90 or 95 miles an hour, with some of the old timers who knew the Speedway better than their own homes.

"That's where Bill got it," a driver would say, pointing to marks on the retaining wall as he casually wheeled the car into a turn. On the track I saw skid marks which apparently had stayed there for years, and on the walls I saw chipped or broken concrete where someone had crashed.

Only one accident occurred during the entire tests, which covered thousands of miles at speeds often well over 100 miles an hour. Offutt was driving about 5 o'clock one morning when he noticed that tires on the right side were badly worn. On the Speedway cars go counter-clockwise and tires on the outside get the most wear. Offutt didn't want to stop to change tires so he decided to reverse direction instead—driving clockwise to shift wear to the other side.

It may have been a combination of changing direction and being tired, but whatever the reason, it happened almost at the same place Hepburn was killed and in very nearly the same way. Going into a turn about 90 Offutt got too close to the lower apron and went off into the infield. The car skidded on the grass, wet from the early morning dew, and hit a bump. One of the worn tires blew out. The car rolled over three times and stopped right side up. Offutt stepped out, his only injury a bump on one knee which had hit the gearshift bracket when the car rolled over. The windshield popped out just as the advertisements said it would, and after changing one tire the car was driven back to the service area.

Offutt said later that he thought he heard the engine backfire and he didn't think he could get through the turn without power if the engine failed. When the tire blew a rear door flew open and the dome light went on, and he couldn't see through the windshield. Then he hit the brakes, and the car rolled. He said he thought he was doing around 112 miles an hour shortly before he went into the turn.

Few problems showed up during the entire two weeks. A couple of shifting forks broke in the manual transmissions, due to bad materials. With better material and a slight change in design there was no further trouble. The automatic transmission proved even more efficient than had been expected; mileage was about equal to the manual shift, due largely to being in positive drive above idling speed.

Except for the shifting forks the only design change resulting from the tests was in the steering geometry, to give better control at high speeds.

Haustein said they tried to hold the cars to a 75-miles-an-hour average for testing the new tubeless tires, which they found to be reasonably satisfactory but still in need of improvement. Tubeless tires were not yet standard equipment.

"There was no real attempt to see how fast the cars would go," Haustein said. "We had no trouble averaging 90 for the laps and we consistently did well over 100 on the straightaway. The fastest lap clocked was 104 miles an hour."

As late as 1956 a Tucker was clocked at 119 miles an hour during the Grand Prix at Sebring, Florida, at night on one of the back stretch straightaways.

When Offutt believed they had all the information they could get from driving on the Speedway they drove the cars back to Chicago, except the one that rolled over which was hauled back in a truck. If Tucker had hoped to impress either SEC or the Justice Department by proving the cars would actually run and back up, he had wasted his time. When Offutt was later called before the grand jury one of the lawyers in the U.S. Attorney's office asked him:

"How were the cars taken to Indianapolis—trucked down or driven down?"

"We drove them," Offutt said.

"Are you sure you drove them down, or did you truck them?"

"We drove them down there," said Offutt.

Even after Offutt had testified on the cars' performance during the Indianapolis tests, the U.S. Attorney's office seemingly refused to believe that Tucker cars could actually be driven.

"How did the cars come back to Chicago?" demanded Robert Downing, Assistant U. S. Attorney.

"Drove them back," answered Offutt.

"All of them?" persisted Downing.

All but one, Offutt told him, the one that rolled over.

"What condition is that car in—it was wrecked, wasn't it?"

"No, I'd say it was damaged," Offutt said. "The car is out at the plant for your inspection. I should think you and the jury would like to go out and see the car, how it went through the accident and there was no more damage to it."

Downing wasn't interested, nor was anybody else in the U.S. Attorney's office.

While the cars were at Indianapolis, Tucker scoured the country trying to find new backing, but the safari after money still hadn't brought any results. Negotiations were started with Howard Hughes, West Coast multimillionaire, and a Tucker was flown out in the Conestoga for Hughes to see and drive. Hughes was more interested in airplanes and movies. Tucker went to see Ed Pauley, oil millionaire, and Winthrop Rockefeller. Many people with money listened to him. At one time Glenn McCarthy, the fabulous oil tycoon from Texas, was reported to be the new Tucker angel. Tucker talked with him several times and finally got the brushoff in the Pump Room at the Ambassador Hotel, where McCarthy was having a party and wouldn't even talk to him again. As reported by *Newsweek*, Tucker said:

"We hit every S.O.B. in the country for money."

At the plant Offutt and his men kept working, hoping somehow to show both the public and the government that their faith in Tucker hadn't been misplaced. Cars were driven to dealers' meetings around the country, where people from the sales department tried desperately to offset the continuing bad publicity that resulted from the investigation.

Around Thanksgiving a dealers' meeting was scheduled for Kansas City, and the Conestoga made its last flight for Tucker. Two cars were to be there; Haustein drove one and the other was loaded on the Conestoga. At Kansas City they ran into a snowstorm and couldn't land, so they turned back and made an emergency landing at Kirksville, Missouri. They unloaded the car, taxied the Conestoga off the blacktop runway onto the sod field and drove the car to Kansas City, where Haustein had beat them in by six hours.

After the dealers' meeting there wasn't time to worry about the Conestoga, which had settled up to its belly in mud by the time Denehie and another pilot went after it the following March. Snow on the control surfaces had weighted down the tail and the front end was sticking up in the air. They jacked it up and put timbers under the wheels, and lined up a row of planks to get back on the runway.

They held the brakes while they revved up the engines, and when they started the wheels ran off the planks and again sank into the mud. It finally took two tractors and a truck with a power winch to get it on the runway, which Denehie said looked like a canal. About the middle of the afternoon they finally got into the air, stopped at Burlington, Iowa, for gas and went on to Chicago, where the Conestoga—along with the Beechcraft—was later sold at auction.

Late in October *Newsweek* reported that forty FBI agents "were inquiring into the activities of the corporation and its officers," and Kup's column in the *Chicago Sun-Times* said "The FBI had stepped into the 'Tucker Case' in order to determine if the mails were used to defraud." Similar reports continued and increased on radio and in newspapers and magazines.

In answer to receivership and bankruptcy suits which were piling up, Tucker made a report to the Federal court in Chicago showing the company still had more than $8,000,000 in assets, including something under $4,000,000 in dealers's notes. Early in December he called a dealers' meeting at the plant in hopes of collecting enough money to keep the company going until SEC and the Justice Department either killed it or gave it a clean bill of health. Neither agency seemed to be in any hurry and time was running out. Some dealers paid their notes, but not enough to be of any real help.

The Reconstruction Finance Corporation had turned Tucker down flat on his application for a loan, even while continuing loans to Kaiser, which were estimated to reach $200,000,000. About the only government agency that maintained any connection with Tucker without squawking was War Assets, which revealed that $125,000 for three months' rent had been paid on the dot November 1.

24

The Last Lap

BEFORE THE FIRST WEEK IN DECEMBER ENDED IT WAS AP-
parent to almost everyone that Thanksgiving hadn't brought
the company much to be thankful for, and the prospects
looked even rougher for Christmas. With all their performance and dash, the hopeful new Tucker automobiles were
on the last lap, and the corporation had troubles that couldn't
be handled in a pit stop.

Not that the company was broke. The balance sheet as of
October 31, 1948, still showed more than $16,000,000 in
assets, including almost $3,000,000 in parts and materials.
Liabilities were well under $2,000,000, and the figure was
only slightly higher in December.

After Thanksgiving holiday, about 300 production workers
were called back and they continued putting together the few
cars for which there were still complete parts. It was the last
hiring and they were kept on only a few weeks. Tucker had
stopped drawing his salary months before and all people who
weren't absolutely necessary were being let out.

Under the increasing pressure of the investigation, more

executives and members of the board of directors were resigning or leaving by request. As money got tighter, arguments became bitter, as in any household. Herbert Morley, director of purchases, resigned, charging Tucker with creating "conditions under which no business can be properly conducted." Morley certainly was right about the conditions, but whether Tucker alone created them was debatable. Cerf resigned from the board, and with him Barnett Faroll, prominent on La Salle Street. Bryce B. Smith of Kansas City, board member and personal friend of President Truman, bailed out.

D. McCall White, special assistant in charge of engineering and testing, left when his six months contract ran out. Most of us in publicity suspected the chief reason Tucker hired White was for the headline "Former Office Boy Hires Ex-Boss," though it may be Tucker actually thought he could hurry the process of getting into production.

Losing so many of his key men was hurting Tucker's prestige, not only with the public but with the dealers, even though they were satisfied with the car. A dealers' committee had been formed, hoping they could save the corporation even if Tucker had to walk the plank.

On La Salle Street many financial men blamed the election, saying money was always tight in election years and that Cohu was stalling to see how the election came out. Negotiations with La Motte T. Cohu of No. 1 Wall Street had been initiated by Tucker in September, but Cohu's option expired without any action being taken.

"If the Wall Street man for President (Thomas E. Dewey) had won, the Cohu plan might have gone through," was the comment on La Salle Street.

As the situation got worse, suits against the corporation multiplied. On December 15 Judge Michael L. Igoe ordered two bankruptcy suits consolidated into a single suit, set a December 22 deadline for the company to file an answer, and set January 4 for a hearing. A few days later newspapers reported that U. S. Attorney Otto Kerner, Jr., had conferred with Hart of SEC and had assigned two assistants to the case. The newspaper stories said Kerner's office had "been checking for possible violation of federal laws."

On January 3, the day before the hearing, Judge Igoe is-

171

sued an order postponing all bankruptcy, liquidation and receivership actions against Tucker for another sixty days. The reprieve started speculation that Nash or Willys was interested, and James D. Mooney, Willys-Overland president, was reported ready to step into Tucker's place. Other reports said Rockelman would succeed Tucker, backed by a dealers group.

In the January issue of *True* magazine there appeared a story which made Tucker feel better. but which was almost lost in the flood of reports on court action, financing troubles and the threat of criminal action by the government. The writer was Ken W. Purdy, *True*'s automotive editor who, the magazine said, had been told to "call it the way you see it and to hell with the advertising angles." His story added Tucker to the legendary giants in automotive history:

" . . . men who never quite got over the thrill they felt the first time they stepped on the gas and felt a good car jump beneath them. These men, the E. L. Cords, the Fred Duesenbergs, the Harry Millers, were simply car-crazy. They were queer for automobiles.

"They built cars for men," Purdy wrote. "The Mercer was such a car, and the Stutz. So was the Cord—if you find one in good shape today, you've still got a hell of an automobile—and so was the mighty Duesenberg, a man's car if one ever rolled down the road. One thing and another (put the depressions of '21 and '31 at the top of the list) killed off these cars, and from the last Cord to the first Tucker, the field for the car engineered to be years ahead of its time was clear. In advanced engineering and high performance the Tucker occupies a rightful place of succession in this noble line."

Purdy drove the Tucker and, like McCahill, said it lived up to its promises:

"The car will do 125 miles an hour. It will deliver 26.2 miles to the gallon of gasoline at 45 m.p.h. It will accelerate from a standing start to 30 m.p.h. in three and a half seconds, from 0 to 60 in ten flat. (For laughs, try that on your present car.) It is the safest car ever built, period."

The tribute in *True* magazine didn't pay off any creditors, or have any appreciable effect on government agencies or on Judge Igoe, who ordered the plant shut down on a maintenance basis January 7, to remain in effect until changed or

172

canceled by the court. Payment of salaries was stopped except to an assistant secretary and the comptroller, who had already resigned.

On February 15 Kerner announced a grand jury would investigate Preston Tucker "and certain aspects of the Tucker corporation." The grand jury was set to open the following Monday and was expected to last thirty days. On the day of this announcement, it was reported that an 800–page confidential report on Tucker had been sent to the Justice Department by SEC.

In Washington at the time, Tucker said the hearing "will provide a welcome opportunity to explain our side of the story." When he got back to Chicago he was still hopeful, and worked night and day with dealers groups trying to save the company. Before the hearing opened a new board of directors was elected, composed entirely of Tucker dealers and distributors. Tucker and four board members had offered their resignations. Those of the board members were accepted, but the new board asked Tucker to stay on as president.

It was a gloomy Monday when the grand jury investigation opened, matching Tucker's feelings as he delivered the first installment of an estimated twenty-five truckloads of records to the District Attorney's office. Kerner had demanded the company's books, engineering data and correspondence since December 1, 1946, and Tucker saw a last chance to show the people in Chicago, at least, that he had built automobiles that would run.

Without a traffic permit or an escort, Tucker, driving a powder-blue 48, led a parade of eight Tuckers which stalled traffic when they pulled up on the Adams Street side of the Federal building in the Chicago Loop.

In the rain, while people crowded around the cars, a few employees who still hadn't given up, opened the front luggage compartments and took out armloads of records, which they carried into Federal building where the grand jury was waiting to start. From the sidewalks and streets people called to him:

"We're with you—we're pulling for you, Mr. Tucker."

With only a handful of officers and directors left, Tucker

173

asked Dan Leabu to pinch-hit as secretary-treasurer until somebody else could be found for the job. Leabu agreed.

Shortly after, there was a telephone call from someone who said he represented a group that was interested in supplying the necessary capital, and wanted to talk with Tucker. Leabu said Tucker was out of the city, but he could represent him, and if the man wanted to check he could call Tucker. The man didn't give his name, didn't say who he represented, but said he would call later.

"A week later the same man called," Leabu said. "Tucker wasn't in so he agreed to see me, but said he wouldn't talk to anybody but me or Tucker. He told me to come alone that afternoon and gave me an address. It was in Cicero."

Haustein, who with Leabu and Offutt was one of the last men still working with Tucker, tuned up one of the cars and had it washed and shined. Leabu took projection charts and graphs showing production schedules over one-, three-, six-, and twelve-month periods: the percentage of completion of production lines; inventories of parts and materials; estimated profits, and the number of employees that would be needed. They set the figure at 2,000 to start, climbing to 15,000 after a year's time.

When he got to the address he found a man at the door of a two-story building who took him to an apartment on the second floor. There he was introduced to a man sitting in a wheelchair with a light blanket over his legs. Leabu said he looked between 45 and 50 years old.

Leabu opened his briefcase and started telling the man what he thought any potential investor would want to know—what their position was now, and what the prospects were for profits on the investment.

"We're not interested in that information," the man in the wheelchair told him. "All we want to know is how many men you're going to hire over the first six months after we put our money in, and what your total employment will be."

"How much can you put in?" Leabu asked. The man told him $10,000,000 or more, whatever they needed. Leabu said he asked the man who his principals were, and the man opened a magazine that was lying on the table and pointed to one of the pictures. (The magazine was the November 28, 1948, issue of *Life,* with a story under the caption "The Chi-

174

cago Rackets'' about the men who were in line to take over the Capone empire.)

"This is the boss," the man said.

Leabu asked him what they wanted for security—stock, someone in the treasurer's office, people on the board of directors?

The man said they didn't want any stock or any positions in the company, and they didn't want any security.

"Then what do you get for your money?" Leabu asked.

"He told me," Leabu said, "that they wanted the right to place a number of their own men in jobs in the plant. I asked him, 'How does this protect your investment?' He said 'We want five percent of your employees to be our men. They can be stock chasers, crib attendants, in the shipping department—anywhere they can move around and meet lots of other workers.

"I still didn't understand until he laid it out for me: they wanted the gambling concession in the plant to sell mutuel tickets, numbers, whatever they were working on at the time. He said they expected a return of a million dollars a year and it would be no different from what was already going on in other plants around the country, with or without the knowledge and consent of the management.

"Just to get out of there in one piece, I said I would talk it over with Tucker, and he told me to be sure no one else knew about it.

"While I was waiting for Pres to get back, I saw a big story in the papers that the Justice Department was all ready to move in on the rackets. In about a week I got another call from the same man. He said the deal was off, that there was too much heat and he would let me know. That was the last I heard from him."

25

A Thumb on
the Scales of Justice

EARLY IN JANUARY OF 1949 TUCKER HAD WRITTEN THOMAS
B. Hart, SEC Regional Administrator, protesting newspaper
stories which he charged originated with SEC. Hart's reply
said that "at no time has this Commission ever furnished or
made available any information to any newspaper or any other
unauthorized sources."

Hart further assured Tucker that the Commission's investigation "has at all times been conducted in a fair and im-
partial manner and in the strictest of confidence." Less than
two months after Hart's letter was received, the biggest and
most sensational automotive story of the year broke in the
Detroit News.

GIGANTIC TUCKER FRAUD CHARGED IN SEC REPORT said the
streamer on the front page of the Sunday paper March 13.

A subhead said, "Car is Called a Monstrosity," and below
it that conspiracy indictments were urged for Tucker and
twelve of his associates. The story was under the byline of
Martin S. Hayden, Washington correspondent for the *News,*
and carried a Washington dateline. Nowhere was the SEC

report referred to as "secret" or said to be considered confidential by SEC or the Justice Department.

In the story Hayden listed and elaborated charges in the report: that Tucker got $759,000 of corporation funds, that claims for the car "were grossly misleading and false," and that all the cars were "hand built." Much of the story, it seemed obvious, came from interviews with early Tucker employees, because references were almost entirely to the first experimental model, the Tin Goose.

Timing couldn't have been better. Detroit readers were following the grand jury in Chicago, worrying that Tucker might become competition and threaten their security. And news was scarce that day.

Editors of the *News* couldn't have been stupid enough not to realize that the story would damage Tucker, perhaps irreparably, and no one could doubt it would influence the grand jury. A grand jury isn't held incommunicado like a trial jury, herded back and forth to hotel rooms by a bailiff. Members go home at night and come back in the morning, and it is only reasonable to expect that they read newspapers, listen to radio, watch television like other people, and talk about things that are going on. The chief occupation of jury members was the investigation of Tucker, and the *Detroit News* story—reprinted and rewritten in countless other papers—would have first claim on their attention. Tucker couldn't have countered the *News'* blast if he had had his own printing presses.

Outside the courtroom opinion grew stronger that the automotive industry was behind Tucker's opposition, and that Senator Ferguson and SEC Commissioner Harry McDonald, another Detroiter, were among those pulling the strings behind the scenes.

The industry may have guffawed publicly, as reported by Tom McCahill, when Tucker was mentioned, but privately they knew that the Tucker performed. They knew from disinterested reports by men whose judgment was unquestioned, and from their own sources inside Tucker's organization. Spies are as inherent a part of the industry as in international diplomacy, and tales of their exploits have become legend.

There was the testimony of men like McCahill and Purdy,

and Detroit's own automotive writers, who a year earlier told their readers what they thought of Tucker's new automatic transmission. One comment most widely heard was that if Tucker ever got into production, it would cost the industry millions for new models that could match the Tucker for horsepower and performance.

When queried about the release of the SEC report, U.S. Attorney Otto Kerner, Jr., expressed amazement and shock and said he had telephoned Alexander M. Campbell, head of the Criminal Division of the Justice Department, and urged him to make an immediate investigation. Kerner said he wanted to learn who was responsible for disclosure of what he said was a "confidential" report. Edmund M. Hanrahan, SEC chairman, told the *Chicago Sun-Times* by telephone, from his home in New York, that he was returning to Washington immediately "to check up on this leak." Hanrahan promised a full investigation to learn how the report became public.

It looked for a time as if the government might ease up on Tucker long enough to check on some of its own officials. If the investigations were made, the answers should have been known to Kerner and Hanrahan within days, or even hours.

Up to the *News* story it was by no means certain that the grand jury would decide Tucker was a criminal and guilty of conspiracy to defraud, and there was a possibility that the jury wouldn't even return an indictment. Tucker and his associates were charged with waste, extravagance and mismanagement, but these would not stand up as criminal offenses.

Moreover, some testimony was favorable to Tucker. Offutt and others told the jury how the cars performed at Indianapolis, and other witnesses refuted accusations that no engineering had gone into the Tucker car. There was sworn testimony that Senator Ferguson was out to "get Tucker," and that McDonald had told associates in a Detroit gold club that the heat against Tucker was terrific, and that automobile officials had followed him into the men's toilet to talk to him about Tucker.

But by piling up witnesses and exhibits, Kerner and his force were convincing the grand jury that the Tucker 48 did not have all the features which were publicized before and after Tucker sold his stock. The mill was grinding inexorably, aided by the flood of adverse publicity following the *News* story.

While the grand jury was still in session Tucker had been lined up for a new blast, even stronger than the first, and like the first it could have been expected to influence the grand jury's decision. Neither Kerner nor SEC could have known how long the grand jury would deliberate.

The new blast was a story in the June 25, 1949, issue of *Collier's* magazine, with the heading both on the cover and inside: "The Fantastic Story of the Tucker Car." It was similar to the one in the *News* but longer, more detailed, and written by one Lester Velie.

Tucker was convinced that the leak to the *Detroit News,* and later to *Collier's,* was deliberate and from the government itself. So he waited impatiently after both SEC and Kerner promised investigations, believing that if he were right and the information was made public, it would end the grand jury hearing.

If the grand jury returned an indictment and the disclosure wasn't made until after the trial started, his attorneys felt sure the trial would end with a motion to dismiss, because both the grand jury and the trial would be a farce if it were proved that the prosecution had its thumb on the scales.

But neither SEC nor the Justice Department ever made the result of their investigations public, if the investigations were made as promised.

Indictment of Tucker and seven of his associates was announced by Kerner June 10, and newspapers across the country carried headlines INDICT TUCKER ON 31 COUNTS— TUCKER, 7 AIDES INDICTED. Of the thirty-one counts in the indictment, twenty-five charged mail fraud, five were on violations of SEC regulations and one on conspiracy to defraud. Rumor was that it might be a year before the defendants were brought to trial, because of a crowded Federal Court docket.

Those indicted along with Tucker were listed as Harold A. Karsten, 58, who had helped promote the deal originally and was squeezed out; Floyd D. Cerf, 60, the broker who handled the stock issue; Robert Pierce, 63, who served most of the time as a consultant without salary; Fred Rockelman, 63, former vice president of Ford and president of Plymouth; Mitchell W. Dulian, 55, one of Tucker's personal friends and sales manager; Otis Radford, 45, who served briefly as comptroller, and Cliff Knoble, 50, advertising manager. Bond was set at $25,000 for Tucker, Cerf, Pierce and Karsten, and at $10,000 each for the rest. If convicted, each of the defendants faced possible penalties totaling 155 years in prison and $60,000 fines.

Tucker branded the charges "silly and ridiculous," and hit back at SEC saying:

"A secret investigation like the one conducted by the Securities and Exchange Commission is likely to upset any company, strong or weak, old or new, and is worse than an indictment."

Tucker was yet to learn that an indictment can be as bad as a conviction, and accomplish essentially the same results. Time alone would finish off Tucker's corporation and his car. Manufacturers were steadily increasing production to meet rising demand, and the government wouldn't hold Tucker's plant idle for a year waiting to find out whether a jury would find him guilty or innocent.

During the hearing Tucker received scores of letters with money and checks enclosed, urging him to keep fighting. One letter from Sidney, Ohio, was written with a pen and addressed "Preston T. Tucker, Chicago, Illinois." The letter said:

Dear Mr. Tucker:

I was just getting ready to buy one of your new cars when the big boys squeezed you out. I wouldn't give up so easy. Why not ask every one in the country to send you a buck? With approximately 160 million in this country you should get $50 million. Here's the first one.

Good Luck

It was signed T. A. L., or the last letter could have been "T."

On the advice of his attorneys Tucker returned letters with checks and money to senders, when the letters had return

180

addresses. The lawyers said they had enough problems already without getting the Post Office Department on their necks too, and probably Internal Revenue besides.

Tucker kept the one letter from Ohio with the dollar bill still attached. It was letters like this which helped him to keep on working long after most of his associates had given up, and strengthened his conviction that the people still believed in him and his car.

26

"Let's Get Down to the Meat"

THE SAME HEADLINES WHICH ANNOUNCED OPENING OF THE Tucker fraud trial October 5, 1949, in Federal Court also revealed that, as far as the corporation was concerned, the trial was over before it started. TUCKER LOSES AUTO PLANT; TRIAL OPENS, said a red streamer in the *Chicago Herald American*. And in the *Detroit Free Press*: TUCKER LOSES PLANT; TRIAL ON.

With variations, headlines around the world told the story to Tucker stockholders and dealers: that the company was out of business before the first witness had been called.

The enemies were winning. The nightmare had started. Tucker saw it outlined in the newspapers:

"Preston Tucker lost his huge war-surplus plant as he and seven associates went on trial for alleged fraud in the $28,000,000 financing of his rear-engined automobile.

"Federal Judge Michael L. Igoe signed an order returning the sprawling $172,000,000 structure on Chicago's South Side to the War Assets Administration.

"The order gives the court-appointed trustees sixty days to

try to sell the ten-year lease on the plant, Tucker's option to buy it for $30,000,000, and the machinery inside the building.''

Igoe's order was curtains for Tucker because there wasn't a chance anyone would put up money while the promoters were on trial, and even less chance that the trial would be over in sixty days. Writers predicted it would be the longest criminal trial since M. L. Annenberg was tried for eleven months in 1939 and 1940 for tax evasion. The whole situation had been rigged so Tucker could not win.

Even if Tucker and his associates were found innocent, the company had already, in effect, been tried and convicted, and the government itself had pronounced sentence: without a plant no Tucker cars would be built. Tucker also had been tried and convicted in print. A condensation of the *Collier's* article appeared in the September issue of *Reader's Digest* and the November *Coronet* carried what looked like a toned-down rewrite of the *News* and *Collier's* stories.

It could hardly be expected that these would not affect the judgment of jurors in the trial, because there would be plenty of time to read them before a panel had been selected.

To Tucker investors the trial would be a farce, but the stage was set, the actors were ready and the show would go on as scheduled. For the government there was Otto Kerner, Jr., 41, soft-spoken and intense, and two assistant attorneys, Lawrence J. Miller, 43, and Robert J. Downing, 34. Also on Kerner's staff were two men from SEC.

Heading the defense battery were William T. Kirby and Frank J. (Spike) McAdams, attorneys for Tucker. The right sleeve of McAdams' coat hung loose, souvenir of the invasion of Leyte when he had been a lieutenant commander in the Navy. Floyd E. Thompson, former Chief Justice of the Illinois Supreme Court, was attorney for Cerf, and defending Pierce was Albert W. Dilling.

There was even a prologue and some comedy relief. When the indictment was returned Kerner sent three deputy U.S. marshals to Tucker's apartment while photographers waited to get pictures of him in leg irons, which the deputies had ready in their car. Tucker had been tipped off and at the time was enjoying the seclusion of the Adler Planetarium. He stayed out of sight until the trial opened, then drove to the

Federal building in a blue Tucker, went to the courtroom with McAdams and posted his $25,000 bond.

For comedy relief there was one government witness, formerly on Tucker's payroll, who stayed in a Loop hotel at government expense throughout the trial. Early in the proceedings he decided Tucker was getting a bum deal and he didn't want any part of it, so he solved the problem in his own way. Every day thereafter he showed up at the courtroom drunk, sure that Kerner wouldn't want him on the stand in that condition. He would weave into the courtroom, put an arm around Miller's shoulder and say:

"How 'bout it, pal, you wanna put me on today?"

Miller would pull away.

"No, no. You come back tomorrow."

It is highly unlikely anybody could have stayed drunk through the four-month trial without getting killed going across the Loop, so the reluctant witness probably at least part of the time just sloshed whiskey around in his mouth in the morning to make a good strong smell. However the witness worked it, he was never called.

On the bench was U.S. District Judge Walter J. La Buy.

Off in a corner near a window in the big courtroom, silent and grim, sat Regional SEC Chief Thomas B. Hart, who three years earlier, almost to the day, had started the series of investigations which already had ended the Tucker automobile. Along La Salle Street brokers said:

"Tom Hart knows more about the Tucker Corporation than any person except Tucker."

They probably were right, because SEC had spent more time investigating Tucker than Tucker had spent trying to build automobiles.

For the first time since the weathered stone Federal building had been opened, the courtroom was wired for sound. The acoustics were so bad, and people directly connected with the trial numbered so many, that they had to have a PA system to hear each other. Microphones were placed by the chair for witnesses, on the judge's bench and on the podium, where attorneys would rant and argue.

As the trial opened, the Reconstruction Finance Corporation was considering Kaiser-Frazer's application for a loan to develop and tool 1951 models, and to finance dealers who couldn't get money to floor plan new automobiles. Before the trial was well under way, RFC had approved loans to Kaiser totaling some $40,000,000.

Kerner's opening statement made the government's case clear—perhaps too clear for Kerner's own good—in that it was patently untenable. He told the jury:

"It is not for us to determine whether the promised automobile was to be five years ahead of its time, whether it was to be the safest automobile in the world or whether it would deliver thirty-five miles per gallon of gasoline. With these things we are not concerned. But this is a criminal case; the matter to be determined by you is whether or not a fraud was perpetrated by these defendants."

Kerner's first moves put him in a position that was going to be hard to defend. While insisting that the government had no interest whatever in merits of the Tucker car, witness after witness was called to testify how the Tin Goose broke down before the World Premiere—how the torque converters to both rear wheels were abandoned, and the Tucker 48 didn't have disc brakes or fuel injection. It looked like Kerner's entire case was riding on the helpless Tin Goose.

I was one of the first witnesses, and when I got back to Chicago to take the stand and saw Tucker again, I could see that he had taken a terrific beating since I had last seen him a few months before. His nerves were on edge and he was depressed, and bitter against the forces and men who had put him out of business before the trial even started. Yet he was at the same time confident that he would be vindicated. No matter how events were against him, nothing could shake his confidence in himself.

I was only on the stand about ten minutes. I testified that I wrote the *Pic* story about Tucker and that so far as I knew it was true. That seemed to satisfy the government and there was no cross-examination.

After I was dismissed I went to Philadelphia. A week or so later I saw a paragraph on an inside page saying that the judge had stopped the trial October 11, allowing a defense motion for a mistrial. For a moment my spirits picked up, but I soon discovered it was only a temporary delay and that Tucker would have to stand a new trial. When I returned to Chicago friends filled me in on what had happened.

* * *

Mark Mourne of Denver, an attorney, Tucker's cousin and former secretary of the corporation, was testifying about the part played by Karsten, one of the defendants, in early promotion of the deal. Mourne was telling about a conversation with Tucker about Karsten (then known as Karatz), and in answer to a question by Miller, he started:

"I told Tucker that Karatz had a criminal record, and that he . . ."

Whatever Mourne was going to say was drowned out as defense attorneys jumped up objecting, and when Judge La Buy finally got them quieted down McAdams moved for a mistrial, asserting that Mourne's testimony would prejudice the jury.

Judge La Buy dismissed Miller's argument that such evidence was necessary to the government, to prove that the defendants had evil intentions when they associated with a man who had a record. The judge said the law had two requirements for admitting such evidence: that there must be similarity of offense and relevancy in point of time, and that this evidence failed to meet either requirement. He likewise overruled instructing the jury to "erase" Mourne's testimony from its mind, to just pretend it hadn't heard him at all, and warned the prosecution not to let it happen again.

One of the first witnesses after the trial resumed was Robert B. Walder, who had worked for Tucker about two months after the stock was sold. Walder said he thought the car was in a "relatively early stage of development," and that he "questioned the fuel economy with that size of power plant."

Under cross-examination he explained that he was talking about the Tin Goose, and not the final Tucker engine at all. It was also established that he brought an engine with him to Chicago which he tried to sell to Tucker, and that he left shortly after Tucker told him he wasn't interested.

"So before you came to Chicago you had an idea that maybe you could sell him that engine?" asked Kirby.

"Yes, I suggested it to Mr. Tucker."

"You came to Chicago and you brought that engine with you?"

"Yes sir," answered Walder.

The witness also identified a letter dated in August of 1947 in which he wrote: "Now, Preston, I will never forget the help back there in New York before the war started. I was pretty well down when you introduced me to that party at Brewsters, through which I have made a deal at Dresser Industries. In fact, I remember that you drove me over to the La Guardia Airport at 1:30 in the morning so I could make the plane and be in Buffalo where I signed up a contract that was highly important to me."

Kirby started to say something about casting bread on the waters, but didn't follow it up. Then Daniel D. Glasser, Karatz' attorney, asked Walder if it was true that he had changed his name legally from Braun-Walder to Walder. He said it was true.

"When you were subpoenaed by the United States government in this case, did they refer to you in the subpoena as Robert Walder alias Robert Braun-Walder?" asked Glasser.

The prosecution objected, saying it wasn't important.

"I think it is important," said Glasser. "They did that in this case to the defendant Karsten. They did it as deliberately as they could. There is no reason why I cannot do it here."

The judge said it could stand, and Glasser repeated his question:

"Did they refer to you as alias Braun-Walder when they subpoenaed you?"

"No," answered Walder.

"They didn't do that?"

"No, sir."

"That is all," said Glasser.

Paul G. Wellenkamp was another of the government's expert witnesses who also belittled the engine in the Tin Goose, saying it had a carburetor instead of a fuel injector. He worked for Tucker about the same time as Walder, and said the only automobile factory he ever worked in was Willys-Overland, where he spent part of two summers while he was still going to school. Wellenkamp proved to be one of Tucker's best witnesses against the conspiracy charge.

"Do you think it was an honest effort in good faith to produce that kind of an automobile?" he was asked.

"Yes, sir, I do," Wellenkamp said.

Along with Walder and Wellenkamp was Carl H. Scheuermann, SEC's expert witness on transmissions, who had worked on the four-speed manual shift but not the automatic. Under cross-examination he, too, fell apart, failing to prove that Tucker lied when he promised a fully automatic transmission.

Throughout the trial the argument came up at intervals over the SEC report, which the prosecution insisted was "secret and confidential," and the defense attorneys said was clearly not confidential because the government had already given it to publications fighting Tucker. At one point during the argument, Judge La Buy said emphatically:

"To permit the SEC to expose the report to the public press and have the District Attorney deny the same right to the defendant shocks the Court's sense of justice, fairness and right."

But throughout the trial defense attorneys couldn't even read the report, much less get a copy for their own use.

After the prosecution went through the "supporting witnesses," men who had worked for Tucker even if only for a short time, Kerner's staff went down SEC's list of dealers, who identified ads, literature and correspondence they had read or received before and after they bought franchises. The government insisted these exhibits were proof of fraud and conspiracy. But under cross-examination witness after witness, even many who were hostile to Tucker personally, gave the same answer when asked if they believed Tucker was conspiring to defraud people who bought stock and franchises.

"Do you believe Mr. Tucker was making an honest effort to get automobiles into production?" they were asked.

One after another answered, "Yes."

When defense attorneys protested that the prosecution was prolonging the trial unreasonably without showing proof of either fraud or conspiracy, they found the court in agreement with them. Early in the trial, reports said much of the government's evidence was admitted "with the reservation that the prosecutors must tie it up later with the general charges of conspiracy," and that some of it might be ruled out later.

"I am just powerless," said Judge La Buy following one protest. "I will have to let it go in. I am getting to be impatient too. I would like to see some concrete case on conspiracy established here."

When the defense objected to the testimony of one witness as irrelevant, Judge La Buy told the prosecution:

"If you have facts, bring them out. I've been very liberal in admitting evidence and allowing you to tie it up later. Now let's get down to cases. If your witness can testify so as to tend to prove a fraud, all right, but let's get down to the meat."

Things were beginning to look up for the defendants, but for the corporation the picture was getting darker daily. As the December winds off Lake Michigan grew colder, it was obvious the plant would need heat for even limited operation, and this was one of the reasons given by Igoe's trustees when they reported that they were "extremely doubtful" that the corporation as a whole could be reorganized.

According to Chicago papers, War Assets told the trustees it would cost $225,000 to winterize the plant and another $115,000 for coal and other cold weather necessities. While the trial droned on the rent piled up, with a quarter of a million back rent already due.

By the time the trial was recessed in December for the Christmas vacation, the prosecution had proved many charges: that there had been waste and extravagance, that mistakes had been made, that various mechanical features had been changed or abandoned, and that features publicized for the first Tucker "Torpedo" weren't present on the 48. But the prosecution hadn't proved either fraud or conspiracy, in the opinion of defense lawyers, who admitted at the same time that the trial wasn't over yet.

Kerner could be expected to save his star witnesses for the last, after the trial reopened in January.

Aspirin,
Cokes and Coffee

DANIEL J. EHLENZ OF WHITE BEAR LAKE, MINNESOTA, WAS one of the stars Kerner had been saving for the finale, and he proved to be one of the defense's best witnesses. Having paid $28,000 for his Tucker distributorship in St. Paul, Ehlenz might reasonably have been expected to be somewhat bitter against Tucker for loss of his investment.

He was exceptionally well qualified as a witness, having visited the Tucker plant frequently since early in 1946 and having one of the finest collections of Tuckerana in the country, outside SEC. His statement in the report covered fifteen pages and reproduced verbatim most of the literature and correspondence from Tucker since the deal started.

Under direct examination Ehlenz testified he had been in the automobile business nineteen years and that he brought along his own lawyer when he bought his franchise. He told of attending meetings in Chicago and Minneapolis, and said he had visited the Tucker plant about once a month, sometimes oftener, up to the middle of 1948 when the last SEC investigation started.

It was his answers to questions about these visits which brought approving smiles from the jury box. Asked if he knew how long the conveyer system was, Ehlenz said he wouldn't know but it was "plenty long," and questioned about what he saw on some of his visits he answered:

"Well, there were several cars in various stages of construction in the Number Four building."

"Do you recall how many?"

"No, I don't, not at that time, but there were several of them."

"Was it five, ten, twenty?"

"I wouldn't recall on that trip because on subsequent trips there were more cars each time."

"When was the next visit you made there?"

"About another thirty days."

"What did you see on that visit?"

"More cars," said Ehlenz.

During this cross-examination by Kirby the jury sat up and looked interested for the first time in weeks. Earlier they had demanded upholstered seats, reasoning that the least the government could do was make them comfortable. Kirby's questioning brought the jury out of a long trance, induced by the hard seats and the hypnotic repetition of the same exhibits and the same dull, endless testimony.

"Was there any act or statement of these defendants," Kirby asked, "other than this question of the delivery of mass produced cars, that would lead you to believe that they were engaged in a conspiracy to defraud, contrary to federal law?"

"I don't know of any," Ehlenz answered.

Asked if he had driven the Tucker car he bought he said yes, he had, that it had over 10,000 miles on it and he had driven it at least five or six thousand. On one trip from St. Paul to Edgerton, Minnesota, he said it did around twenty miles to the gallon.

"You have observed the performance of the car?" Kirby asked.

"Yes."

"Did it have good acceleration, Mr. Ehlenz?"

"Yes, very good."

"I was asking you about the speed you had driven the car upon the open road, Mr. Ehlenz. What about that?"

"I never had the throttle open."

"About how fast have you gone in it?"

"Probably ninety-five miles an hour."

"Does the car ride well, Mr. Ehlenz?"

"Yes, it rode well."

"Does it perform, in general, well?"

"Very well."

"When you say very well, what do you mean, Mr. Ehlenz?"

"Well, I had never driven another car that performed like that," Ehlenz said.

It was likewise cross-examination which deflated the astronomical figures used by Kerner and SEC to show that Tucker and his associates had received huge personal benefits at the expense of Tucker Corporation.

Tucker's net gain, said headlines early in January, was more than half a million dollars, while the other seven defendants had taken the corporation for another million. The witness was Joseph A. Turnbull, of SEC's Boston office, who described himself as an "accountant investigator," a sort of financial super sleuth.

Turnbull was the prosecution's last witness, and for days had been referring to long columns of figures compiled by himself and five or six assistants over months of investigation in Chicago and Ypsilanti.

The SEC had placed Cerf's gain at $2,443,000 from handling the Tucker stock issue and it looked as if Cerf had become a millionaire overnight until his attorney, Floyd Thompson, started cross-examination of Turnbull.

"Mr. Turnbull," said Thompson, "will you get the exhibit, the check that was paid to Floyd D. Cerf for $2,443,000 that you said he got from Tucker Corporation?"

"I didn't refer to any check," said Turnbull.

"Will you get the satchel in which the money was carried over?"

Miller objected and the court sustained him.

"Did he ever get $2,443,000 from the Tucker Corporation?" persisted Thompson. "Yes or no?"

"In effect, yes," said Turnbull.

"I move to strike the answer as not responsible and I disclaim it," said Thompson.

Over objection by Miller the judge said the question could stand, and Thompson again demanded of Turnbull:

"Did it pay out the money? Yes or no? Did the Tucker Corporation ever pay out $2,433,000 in relation to the stock transaction?"

After considerable sparring, in which Turnbull evaded answering either "yes" or "no," Thompson asked:

"The $2,433,000 that you spoke about was never in the hands of the Tucker Corporation, was it?"

"Never," said Turnbull.

"And it was never paid out by the Tucker Corporation?"

"Yes."

"What do you mean by 'yes'?" asked Thompson.

"I mean yes, it never was."

Thompson asked the witness if he knew there were 632 securities dealers who marketed the stock, and if he knew that a commission of 70 cents a share was paid for selling it and that neither Cerf nor Tucker ever saw the money paid out in commissions. Turnbull said he didn't know how many dealers were involved. Thompson finally asked him:

"You don't mean to say that Floyd D. Cerf ever saw such money, or ever had it in his hands or in his bank account or it was in any way in his control?"

"No," answered Turnbull.

Cutting down the figures SEC had used against Cerf made all SEC's figures suspect, and defense attorneys tore Turnbull's testimony to shreds under continued hammering cross-examination.

Two minor examples were enough to show the jury how SEC's men estimated net profits and built up a staggering total of more than half a million dollars Tucker was alleged to have received as "benefits." These examples were automobiles sold by Tucker to the corporation, the first a Cadillac for which he got $2,985.

"Did you check with the Cadillac Motor Car Company of Chicago to learn whether Mr. Tucker had, on or about March 24, 1947, paid them for a Cadillac automobile $3,394.78?" asked Kirby. "Did you check that with them?"

"No," said Turnbull.

"So that as far as that item is concerned, how much money in pocket from that sale did Mr. Tucker make, do you know?"

"I don't know," said Turnbull.

"He made none?"

"I don't know," repeated Turnbull.

It was the same story with a 1947 Ford, bought for $1,763 and sold to the corporation for $1,763.

One of the big figures in Tucker's total was $100,000 he was allowed for expenses in early promotion of the deal, paid to him in "B" or founder's stock, much of which already had been allocated to Tucker's associates before the "A" stock was ever sold. This was described clearly and accurately in the prospectus.

Another item was a check for $75,000, deposited with an Oak Park bank by the corporation as security for a loan to Tucker, and covered by "B" stock and other collateral.

"Was this check ever cashed by Preston Tucker?" asked Kirby.

"No, it was just used," Turnbull said.

"But it was not cashed by him?"

"That is right."

"Well," said Kirby, "it stood there four days, then it came back to the corporation. Is that right?"

"That is right, yes."

"And then it went back into corporation funds?"

"Yes, sir," Turnbull said.

"Did the corporation lose any money on that transaction?"

"No."

"They did not lose a cent on it, did they, the Tucker Corporation?" demanded Kirby.

"No," Turnbull said.

Item after item, through page after page of testimony, Kirby and the witness went down the list of payments to Tucker, and the questioning finally ended up with an argument over cost of the twin-engine Beechcraft plane which Tucker bought and sold to the corporation. Turnbull at one time set the figure paid to Tucker at $57,283, and under questioning conceded that $2,238 was for insurance already paid on the plane.

Summarizing the totals testified to by Turnbull under direct-examination, Kirby asked him:

"You are not here suggesting these figures are figures of monies fraudulently taken, are you?"

"Not exactly, no."

"You have not indicated any fraud in them, have you?" Kirby asked.

"Well, that Beechcraft item is questionable," said Turnbull. During hours of questioning, the figure for cost of the plane to the corporation wandered between $15,000 and $100,000, and Turnbull explained that it all depended on how you handled it from an accounting standpoint.

As Kirby ended his cross-examination of Turnbull, over figures compiled through months of work by teams of SEC accountants, the argument boiled down to one indictment of Tucker: Turnbull didn't like the Beechcraft transaction, through which Tucker might or might not have made as much as $15,000.

The biggest surprise in the entire trial came after the closing arguments, after Miller told the jury:

"It doesn't make any difference what their intent was when they started out. They made misrepresentations of what they had. Read the pack of lies in their ads and remember what they had and what they didn't have in the way of an auto."

Downing continued the charge:

"The only thing he (Tucker) designed was a tremendous scheme to defraud. He wanted the public's money for nothing and that's what the public got—nothing."

Kerner himself summarized the prosecution's case:

"Did these defendants tell the truth or did they lie to the public? I trust you will find all are guilty."

Defense attorneys didn't answer the tirades. Instead, Cerf's attorney, Floyd Thompson, told the court his client would rest without offering any defense testimony. The government had proved no offense, Thompson said, so there could be no defense. Other defense attorneys joined him and the last was Kirby, who said:

"Tucker rests."

* * *

Judge La Buy's instructions to the jury stressed the importance of proof of intent, and he said the failure to mass produce automobiles was not in itself proof of intent to defraud—that good faith must be considered a "complete defense." Later that same night the jury asked that the judge's instructions be read to them again. The eight defendants were hopeful as they left the courtroom to wait for the verdict in their homes, hotel rooms or in downtown bars. Tucker waited at home.

"I'm in a daze," he said. "It seems like a nightmare. I've never gone through anything like this before."

At 9:13 Saturday night there was a false alarm when a deputy U.S. marshal answered a knock on the door from inside the jury room. An arm reached out with an empty thermos and a voice asked him to get it filled with hot coffee, and please bring some aspirin and a dozen bottles of Coca-Cola.

At 3:07 Sunday afternoon, January 22, there was another knock from inside the jury room. The jury had been out twenty-eight hours and thirty-five minutes, and had deliberated seventeen hours and seven minutes. By this time the defendants had returned and the courtroom was jammed with spectators. Tension rose during a delay of several minutes while court attendants combed the corridors and the men's room looking for Pierce, who had wandered out of the courtroom a few minutes before. The jury filed into the courtroom at 3:30.

"Have you arrived at a verdict?" asked Judge La Buy.

"Yes, we have, Your Honor," answered the foreman, handing a sealed envelope to the deputy clerk. For the first time since the trial opened there was complete silence. The clerk read the verdict:

"We, the jurors, find the defendants (he slowly read the eight names, beginning with Tucker) not guilty."

Judge La Buy walked into his chambers without a word as clerks called for order. They were wasting their efforts.

Tucker was surrounded by his wife, his mother and three sons. Wives hugged and kissed their husbands and defendants pounded each other on the back. Anything that might have been said was drowned out by cheers from the crowded courtroom. The noise carried down to the first floor, where startled guards loosened their guns and rushed up to the sixth floor.

Each of the defendants shook hands with every member of the jury, and one woman juror was crying hysterically.

Several days after the trial Kirby got a call from one of the jurors, who said Kerner had called them into his office to explain their verdict. Kirby said the action was unethical, totally uncalled for and almost without precedent. The juror who called Kirby asked his advice.

"I told him," said Kirby, "you don't have to explain your decision to anybody until the Last Judgment."

Tucker was vindicated but the corporation was gone.

_____ *Part Three*

Behind
the Headlines

28

The Case
Against Tucker

PROSECUTION OF TUCKER WAS BASED LARGELY ON THE "SE-cret and confidential" SEC report which was disowned by the prosecution itself, and was described in court by a U.S. attorney as "wild gossip, conjecture, opinion, you might call it almost anything . . . it is entirely hearsay."

Yet that report was the beginning of a myth which persisted and grew after the trial was over. Like the report, the myth is a fantastic and unbelievable mixture of accusations, exaggerations, half truths and lies, magnifying Tucker's mistakes and ignoring his very real accomplishments.

In the opinion of many it was the automotive industry that was behind the powerful combination of forces which put Tucker out of business. Yet there was never proof, and if there had been it would have been too late to repair the damage to Tucker. The immediate cause of his collapse was the government itself, yet it is the business of SEC to investigate corporations, and the responsibility of the Justice Department to prosecute where wrongdoing is charged.

There were men in government who overstepped their authority, and by the record broke their own laws, to finally destroy Tucker's enterprise. Yet the defection of a few officials cannot be used to indict government itself. Nor can laws be condemned because on occasion there is distortion in their enforcement to cause injustice.

Tucker himself shouldered part of the blame, admitting after the trial that he had made serious mistakes which left him vulnerable to attack. To a degree he accepted fouls as part of the game, and he acknowledged that government is like business on a bigger scale, with ideals and objectives temporarily in the hands of individuals.

But at the time, to Tucker, the SEC was an enemy agent trying with all the resources of government to discredit everything that was being done to promote the automobile.

It was SEC's contention that Tucker had sold both stock and franchises by misrepresentation, and that dealers had been told the car was already engineered and ready for production.

To build up its case the Chicago SEC office sent out teams of investigators. Few if any of these had any knowledge or experience in the automotive field, but all were armed with a list of questions prepared by the Chicago office.

Two investigators from the Forth Worth regional office interviewed dealers in Dallas. A microphone had been concealed in the office, and in another room a commercial recording firm transcribed the entire interviews. In the background are sounds of hammering, automobile horns, telephones ringing and people knocking on doors. And in the records is convincing evidence of SEC's single-minded determination to destroy Tucker. Because none of the testimony favorable to Tucker, which unquestionably was duplicated in interviews across the nation, could be found in the final SEC report.

The story of one dealer who bought a franchise, as recorded in one interview, is generally the story of most of the Tucker dealers—they read or heard about the automobile, they got in touch with Tucker or his associates, and bought a franchise.

"Their whole story as far as the franchise was concerned,"

one dealer told an investigator, "was that if, as and when they ever build automobiles on the basis which they expected to build, that for the town I live in they had set a quota of 50 cars.

"However, there was no guarantee that I would ever receive these cars at all, not even one car. In fact, the expression was used that it was strictly a roll of the dice, that if they build cars why we'd probably roll the seven, and if they rolled craps we'd just crap out together. That if cars were made that it would be just as much of a risk as rolling the dice, because if they ever built cars we would probably make money together, and if they never built an automobile, all I bought was this piece of paper here called a franchise."

Excerpts from the recordings show some of the answers which SEC ignored when its final report was written. It was during the Texas State Fair that one dealer told how the car performed:

"We drove this automobile that we have down here from Chicago and it's terrific. I had occasion to be in Chicago the other day and of course I went out to the factory and was talking to one of the officials there. He said: 'Well, come on now, give us the facts as you see them. We think we've got something that is dynamite, but what is your honest opinion?'

"And I told him just this—that this car is remarkable. It is an amazing automobile. It performs better than any car I have ever had the pleasure to drive, and as far as I am concerned, this was it. This car could be merchandised just as fast as they could turn them out. They wouldn't have to make any changes. They wouldn't have to make any changes. We didn't have a bit of trouble coming down, we got remarkable performances on it and I swear it's something . . . that it's difficult to believe. It's like a dream car. This car, it's just terrific and as I say, I am not a novice in the automobile business."

The dealer was asked about the report that the car wouldn't back up, and he said they had to prove that it could at every service station where they stopped. The investigator asked about gasoline mileage, and he answered: "We figure something like 22 miles to the gallon all the way down, and sometimes we were getting almost 30 miles to the gallon.''

The question returned again and again to the hydraulic torque converters, which the SEC man kept calling ''conversions,'' to disc brakes and fuel injection. The Texas dealer was getting fed up, and asked the SEC man if the commission had anything to do with newspaper and magazine stories that the Tucker wasn't a legitimate car and had an Oldsmobile motor in it. (The October 25, 1948 issue of *Newsweek* carried a story on stockholder and dealer suits featuring two widely publicized reports: that the first Tucker Torpedo was actually a hand-reconstructed Oldsmobile, and that Tucker ''used company funds to buy a home near Bogotá, Columbia.'')

The SEC man was outraged and said: ''I tell you and you can take this for granted: that the SEC has never and never will, is not now and never will, issue any statements to the newspapers about this Tucker car or any other investigation until its case is concluded, until it has all the facts, until it is ready to proceed in court.''

If the Fort Worth SEC man passed the Texas dealers' comments on to the Chicago office they were ignored. because none of the interviews made in Dallas were in the SEC report.

However, the report repeated and amplified accusations that the first experimental model—the Tin Goose—was a rebuilt Oldsmobile. Page after page of figures and tables showed how Tucker had profited personally by $750,000, and others had clipped the corporation for another million. And it was here that another lie, widely publicized by SEC, originated, and finally became part of the Tucker myth:

That ''actually, Tucker had not contributed one penny to the enterprise.''

SEC claimed that when Tucker blamed his major troubles on the government he was overlooking his own mistakes, which might have been valid if it hadn't been for the government's treatment of Kaiser-Frazer under similar—often identical—circumstances.

The mostly widely accepted explanation for the relentless campaign against Tucker was that the commission had burned its fingers on Kaiser and wasn't taking any more chances. Kaiser's first offering in 1945 had been cleared in a single day and was sold largely on Henry Kaiser's personal prestige and early publicity, which announced a revolutionary low-price ''peoples' car'' with front drive and torsion suspension.

Long before Tucker was even indicated, it was public knowledge that Kaiser had failed to reach any of his announced major objectives. Kaiser-Frazer stock never paid a dividend, yet when the company failed there was no public investigation of what Kaiser had done with $54,000,000 of stockholders' money, why he needed more money, or where the car was he had promised when he sold his stock.

While Tucker was being tried, Kaiser applied for and got a heavy RFC loan to develop and tool new models, including one to sell for ''less than the present low-priced models.'' Senator J. William Fulbright of Arkansas protested that Kaiser had been promising such a car ever since he set up shop, but RFC brushed him off. Another whopping RFC loan went to finance Kaiser dealers who could no longer get money from finance companies and banks, and there wasn't an audible protest from SEC.

Without departing from the Tucker story for the sake of a long dissertation on Kaiser, it seems only fair to make a few comparisons, and the first logical one is publicity, which was the chief basis for the government's case against Tucker.

Tucker's early publicity was modest compared with Kaiser's opening splurge, which was handled by Carl Byoir & Associates. An early release annoucned ''Torsionetic suspension, an entirely new development,'' on all four wheels, yet Kaiser ended up with coil springs in front and leaf springs in the rear. Kaiser first announced a front-drive car to sell for $500, but before the deal was even well started it was announced the $500 car was out, but the Kaiser ''Special'' would sell ''well under $1,000.''

Byoir was still stoking the fire when Kaiser sold his second stock issue in 1946, displaying two hand-built front-drive cars in a lavish show at the Waldorf, complete with dinner music,

205

models and movie stars. Salesmen took 467 orders for new
cars in the first two hours and 1,000 the first day. Engineers
said in tests the front drive experimental cars were failures
and—like the Tin Goose—were abandoned.

Succeeding releases in newspapers and automotive and science magazines showed details of the new suspension system,
and told of new engine designs which would make the Kaiser
an entirely new car. What Kaiser ended up with was nothing
more than another automobile—what in an earlier era was
called an "assembled car," when almost anyone could become a manufacturer by finding sources for his parts, building or having a body built, and putting his emblem on the
radiator shell.

Even the long promised low-priced Kaiser finally turned
out to be the "Henry J," which was no more than a Kaiser-
designed body and frame, with standard parts and a Willys
engine. Kaiser's ultimate collapse was in the cards when he
switched to conventional design, which Tucker had insisted
throughout could never compete with established manufacturers.

If Kaiser had been indicted because the car which sold his
stock wasn't the car he finally built he might be in jail yet—
if SEC had been as tough on him as it was on Tucker.

Like Tucker's first "589" engine, Kaiser's various experimental engines apparently didn't make the grade, because he
bought the Continental engine plant in Detroit, just as Tucker
later bought Aircooled Motors. The main difference was that
Tucker got an engine which performed, while the Kaiser engine was obsolete before he started. SEC never explained
why it was O.K. for Kaiser to buy an engine plant, but wrong
for Tucker.

When Tucker was charged with fraud in selling his stock,
Kaiser had admitted buying $2,500,000 worth of his own
stock when a third issue was offered in 1948, trying to
bolster a sagging market. There was a minor rhubarb at
the time, but SEC did little or nothing about it, perhaps
figuring Kaiser had squared accounts when the issue fell
flat on its face and he was stuck with 186,000 shares of
his own stock.

The SEC was quick to follow up Ferguson's charge that
Tucker was a crook because he hired some former War Assets

people. Yet there was no great excitement when, about the time Kaiser bought Willys, John W. Snyder, former Secretary of the Treasury, went with Willys as vice president nine days after leaving his job with the government. One senator charged Snyder was among "former government officials who, in their official capacity, failed to adequately protect the government's interest," referring in part to the many huge RFC loans made to Kaiser. But SEC didn't follow it up, and the Justice Department didn't charge in and call a grand jury to hear the evidence.

The Tucker car, said SEC was "an untested, unproved conglomeration of highly questionable engineering ideas," yet it is probable that any one of the fifty Tuckers would outperform the last supercharged Kaisers built in 1954, six years later.

What are the real facts in the government's case against Tucker? When the SEC called the Tucker car a "monstrosity" was it willful distortion of fact, an honest mistake or only a difference of opinion?

One section of the report listed all the design features which had been publicized since Tucker first announced his new automobile. It was true some of the features had been abandoned; some were believed impractical, not developed far enough, or too expensive for production.

But the report lumped them all together with a paragraph which said: "Convincing proof that each and every one of the foregoing representations was false and misleading . . . ," and among the "each and every one" were the following:

Rear engine. 166 horsepower, flat opposed 6-cylinder engine located below the level of passengers. More power for the weight of the car than any volume production engine ever built. *This was true and could not have been disproved by any automobile authority in the world.*

All four wheels are independently sprung for more safety and comfort. *This was not a matter of opinion; it was fact that could have been verified by any teen-age hotrodder.*

The driver's seat is in the center, with the first real

provision for seeing out since dashboards were given back to the carriage makers. *The same paragraph said Tucker would move the steering wheel to its accustomed place on the left side if people wanted it there.*

The engine can be taken out in thirty minutes by a mechanic who hasn't one hand tied behind him, Tucker says, and in ten minutes if he is on piece work. *In a demonstration at the plant three mechanics took the engine out, replaced it and the car was driven away in 18 minutes.*

Driving lights mounted on the fenders will follow curves in the road, while a fixed Cyclop's Eye center light directs a beam straight ahead. *The lights were reversed, with the center light turning and the fender lights fixed, but the result was the same.*

The laminated glass windshield is enclosed in sponge rubber, too, and mounted so that a hard blow from within will eject it in one piece. *This was demonstrated in an unscheduled accident when Eddie Offutt rolled over during tests at the Speedway.*

A husky 24-volt electrical system, with capacity for any emergency, is the same type used on war planes. *Tucker finally had to settle for six volts because even 12-volt accessories weren't available, but within a few years the entire industry went to 12 volts.*

The Tucker 48 will be the latest in driving simplicity, with no controls in the floor except the brake and foot throttle. *This was true with the automatic transmission, which was planned for production.*

The Torpedo is designed to cruise continuously at 100 miles per hour and will do 130 or better. *The Tucker was proved repeatedly to cruise easily at 100 and had been unofficially clocked at well over 120.*

To Tucker these charges were so ridiculous that he wouldn't even discuss them. During the trial a former associate ran into him one night at the Illinois Athletic club and asked him what had happened, what went wrong? He said Tucker told him:

"I tried to build it too big and too fast. And I took the advice of a lot of old men."

Long after the trial, when enough of the missing pieces had been found to put the picture together, Tucker had another answer which, while it didn't change anything, made him feel better over what had happened to his stockholders and dealers. He said:

"We were jobbed."

_____ *29*

Was the Tucker
Any Good?

IN DECEMBER, 1956, WHEN TUCKER WAS IN THE HOSPITAL
at Ypsilanti, a letter came to him from Bill Hamlin of Ontario, California. The letter started:

Dear Sir:

Car #14 has nearly 120,000 miles on it and, since such
an automobile isn't available yet (tho this one is nearly
eight years old) I hope you will be able to assist me in
obtaining a pair of headgaskets, for I expect to thoroughly overhaul it some time this next year. I prefer the
steel-insert type over copper, due to the aluminum blocks
and heads.

I do not expect undue trouble in obtaining other parts—
unless you know of an "over-haul kit" available—the
gaskets will take care of the problem. The engine hasn't
been apart—not even a valve job yet.

The car is performing beautifully and attracts so much
attention, I take much pride in maintaining it so. It consumes three quarts of oil per thousand miles, and has a

valve lifter that "sounds off" now and then, so I wish to eliminate these conditions.

I have never owned so thrilling an automobile. After all these years—it still possesses more of what I expect in a family vehicle than any car on the market today, regardless of price. Though it has a few things I wish were different, it has the "mostest that I like the best-est."

I certainly wish that the Corporation had had the chance that Kaiser enjoyed—(and thoroughly muffed up)!

Can you give an old "Tucker Pilot" any hope for a *new* Tucker some of these days? Certainly hope there is a chance for an American-built, *Air-cooled*, rear-engine job in the books!

Another letter from Hamlin told of taking his Tucker to a quarter-mile drag strip at Pomona in 1954 when, he said, the stock car record was held by an Olds "88" doing 78.8 through a standing start. One paragraph said:

Our Tucker (1948 and "tired" by Tucker's standards) went thru repeatedly at 82 m.p.h. (*Starting in 2nd gear,* as I had been warned that 1st gear was too severe with the rear-wheel traction of no slip, which might shear an axle.) Anyhow—it convinced everyone there that *the Tucker had it over any Stock Car* up to 1955.

There are still Tucker drivers who can give firsthand testimony to the car's performance and one of the best qualified is Nick Jenin of Fort Lauderdale, who with ten Tuckers has the largest collection in the country. Jenin tells of driving one back to Florida in 1954 after buying it from a dealer in Chicago for $6,500.

"This car was in storage seventeen months and it was its first trip when I got it," Jenin said. "I didn't check the ignition or the plugs, nobody knew how the valves were set up. I just bought it and drove it out; put air in the tires and checked the oil, and hoped the car would make it. I had my wife follow me in a brand new Cadillac Fleetwood so if the damn thing broke down we could leave it.

"We stopped for gas every 200 miles or so, put fourteen

211

or fifteen gallons in the Cadillac and eight or nine in the Tucker. We drove the same route and had the same mileage and we stayed together on the road, about half a mile apart.

"It was a red car and attracted a lot of attention, and north of Atlanta some kids in a '54 Buick Roadmaster needled me for about ten miles. When we hit that straight stretch about thirty-five miles long, I stepped on it. The speedometer showed 110. The kids finally caught up when I stopped at a gas station, and they said they were doing 105 when I left them."

Jenin said this is his favorite Tucker and he has driven it to Chicago and back five times; that it now registers 63,400 miles and still has the original engine, and nothing has ever been done to it.

"You don't need power steering and you don't weave," he said. "Before power steering came in a lot of my friends who drove the Tucker complained that the steering didn't feel right. After they got used to power steering they never complained about the Tucker again.

"The timing has to be right for fuel economy, but when it's right I would say that it does twenty-four miles to the gallon without any trouble. It will take off and go in sand without slipping. Take a Cadillac or a Buick and the rear end will lift. The engine has tremendous torque and you have to be careful starting.

"If you know how to drive a Tucker properly it will run forever. If you goose it, you're gone."

Going more than 100,000 miles without new rings or a valve job was no great surprise to Tucker, and it was no surprise whatever to John L. Burns, chief experimental engineer of Aircooled Motors, who headed the job of getting the engine ready for mass production in the Chicago plant.

The main reason for the Tucker engine's almost unbelievable performance was that it was originally laid out with the possibility in mind that it would be used in an automobile, Burns said, and with its high torque at low engine speed, it felt as if it were coasting all the time.

"Basically it was the same Army-approved airplane and helicopter engine that was good for 1,500 hours without an overhaul. That is the equivalent of 150,000 miles in an automobile, and that engine could be run wide open all day."

While the Syracuse plant was working on the last order, engineers worked the engine over again to make it air-cooled, retaining various features Tucker had added including the flywheel, bell housing and other parts needed for automobile use. They called the new job "the ultimate Tucker engine."

"We took the original engine and added a blower and a shroud for cooling," Burns said. "It has the same bore and stroke (335 cubic inches) and there was a rubber-mounted Sirocco type fan turning with the crankshaft. It was fourteen inches in diameter with sixty-four blades, and it pushed enough air to cross the desert in the daytime. It was test run up to 110 degrees and still operating perfectly."

The engine weighed 525 pounds with all the accessories, and had pulled more than 200 horsepower on the dynamometer. Test work was completed and the engine was on a stand, ready for installation in a green Tucker, when the trustees moved in and stopped all Tucker operations.

But no matter how well the 50 Tuckers performed, if they were no more than hand-built cars as SEC claimed, they might have challenged Maseratis and Ferraris and it still wouldn't have meant anything.

Could the Tucker have been built in mass production, and still had the same performance as the first pilot models?

At Tucker's request the Syracuse plant made an exhaustive analysis to supplement the corporation's own figures, going through the entire automobile part by part with cost figures for everything that went into it. Their figures, Burns said, showed the Tucker could have been built and sold profitably in the same price range as the Buick Roadmaster: about $2,700 stripped, or around $3,000 fully equipped. With 200 horsepower it should have run rings around the Buick, so competition shouldn't have been any problem.

Some changes were planned to lower manufacturing cost, and insure reliability. Springing was to be changed until rubber companies had the suspensions perfected, and the manual shift transmission was to be simplified until the automatic was ready.

Total weight was about 3,600 pounds, and it actually had

213

more horsepower per pound of weight than any stock car in America.

While Lester Velie, in the *Collier's* story, was quoting SEC and the trustees that Tucker couldn't build an automobile, the trustees were still waiting for an independent report from a Chicago engineering firm, Stevenson, Jordan & Harrison, which was dated July 25, about a month after the *Collier's* story ran.

Their findings largely confirmed both the corporation's and Aircooled's cost analyses, setting retail price at $3,289 and the selling price to distributors at $2,302. This pricing, said the report, "contemplates the car as it is now designed. The cost could be reduced by simplifying the construction in several ways."

Cost estimates were based on use of the air-cooled engine which, the report said, would cost approximately $25 less to build and would be about 100 pounds lighter.

The California Tucker owner who so ardently hoped for an American-built, air-cooled, rear-engine automobile should welcome Chevrolet's new "Corvair," which may be as close to an air-cooled Tucker as he will ever come.

And critics, both in and out of government, who derided the Tucker as impractical and a "monstrosity" will find a tougher target in General Motors, because Corvair specifications list many design features which are close to identical. The differential is integral with the engine and transmission, as in the Tucker, and—like the Tucker—drives independently sprung rear wheels through "U" joints.

People who didn't like the location of the Tucker's gas tank can make the same complaint with the Corvair, which has the filler cap in the crown of the left front fender, and the spare tire is likewise stowed in the front luggage compartment.

While the engines are far from identical, the Corvair's is similar to the Tucker's in that it is a flat opposed six, largely aluminum, lists carburetors instead of fuel injection, and is designed to burn regular gasoline.

Devotees of the "straight stick" may complain of the Corvair's three-speed manual transmission (the Tucker had four speeds), but with the trend increasingly toward automatics, the complaints probably will be few and minor.

About the only similarity in the automatic transmission is that both use planetary gears. Chevrolet's probably will have better getaway, with its torque converter where the first Tucker jobs used a fluid coupling, but the Tucker automatic may still surpass it in economy, because of the design feature which put it in positive gear immediately above idling speed.

Chevrolet's new entry in the rear-engine field will unquestionably be superior to the first Tuckers mechanically, with the time spent in development and GM's tremendous resources for research and testing. Whether it can outperform the Tucker may be open to argument until someone (and this is bound to happen) puts them together in a race or timed runs.

In weight-to-horsepower ratio the Tucker was ahead. The Corvair's 140-cubic-inch engine is rated at 80 hp, which figures 30 pounds per horsepower, with its overall weight of 2,415 pounds. The Tucker—with its air-cooled engine rated at 200 hp and overall weight 3,600 pounds—would have had 18 pounds per horsepower.

Corvair's promised "power kit" and new four-speed transmission should narrow the gap substantially in weight-to-horsepower ratio, and make it the nearest to a true sports car in its entire field. While the power kit officially boosts horsepower from 80 to 95, it probably will be well over 100, with Chevrolet's traditional reputation for understatement.

Beyond increased horsepower, the four-speed transmission isn't likely to raise top speed appreciably, if at all. But in the hands of drivers who have a feel for automobiles it should have satisfying flexibility and terrific getaway, with a unique appeal for people who have learned to understand and appreciate sports car performance.

Except for the Corvair's narrower tread (54 inches) and six-cylinder engine, it is close mechanically to the car Tucker was working on the second round. He planned an air-cooled opposed four with 130 horsepower, and a standard tread for a combination sports car and utility vehicle.

Tucker was never a bigot judging the design and performance of automobiles, and there can be no possible question that he would have given the Corvair his enthusiastic approval without even seeing it, on the strength of its specifications alone.

For anybody who may still think the Tucker was something of a freak, it was a six-passenger four-door sedan that was longer, lower and more powerful than any standard American automobile yet on the road at that time. And if there is still any question about its performance there are enough Tuckers around the country to find out. In addition to Jenin's ten in Florida and Hamlin's No. 14 in California, there were (at last report) three more in California in top shape. There are some in museums around the country; several around Chicago, some in Minnesota, Michigan and New York. There was one—rusting, shabby and neglected—on a used car lot in Miami with a $6,500 price tag.

If you can talk a present Tucker owner into letting you try one out, or at least giving you a ride, you can check their speed, getaway, fuel economy and ride.

The Tucker you try may have a sagging suspension arm, if it has some of the early ones that weren't made right and haven't been replaced. The engine may be rough at idling speed, if it has the original high-lift camshaft, or the carburetion isn't right. If it has a manual gear shift—and only two or three were built with automatics—it may shift hard, if the switches are corroded or there are leaks in the vacuum lines.

But if the Tucker you try is in any kind of shape at all, it will still give whatever you're driving now one hell of an argument on the open highway.

30

What Went Wrong?

THERE COULD BE NO VALID CRITICISM OF THE TUCKER'S PER-
formance, and the government's own investigation showed it
could be built competitively. And there was an assured market, proved by experienced dealers and by people who bought
some $2,000,000 worth of accessories just for a chance to
buy the car.

So why the continued and determined opposition from the
government, and the pretended surprise when Tucker needed
more money? This was spelled out clearly in the prospectus,
warning that failure to obtain such funds might result in
"substantial losses" to investors.

At the time it was charged the deal was born in nightclubs
and cocktail lounges, proving it was a swindle from the start.
Cocktail lounges played their part, it is true, but chiefly in
Washington, where no one in his right mind makes a confidential call through a hotel switchboard, or talks in a room
that might be bugged. If part of the deal was made in saloons,
Tucker had distinguished company.

It will be said the guy tried and missed, so what of it? Who cares? If it were only the story of Tucker there could be little argument. But it is also the story of a lot of ordinary people who bought stock and franchises. Some were gamblers and shrugged off their losses. Many were not and came to suffer hardship, even poverty. There was at least one suicide. And there was a smaller group of skilled and devoted men, who accomplished near miracles trying to make Tucker's dreams into reality.

It is to these people, if to any, that some explanation seems due. People one columnist called ". . . gullible souls . . . misguided and accepting fallacies with something approaching religious fervor." Throughout history such people have followed men who believed unshakably in themselves, who became prophets of a sort—and Preston Tucker, with all his faults, was one of these.

Probably the deciding factor against Tucker was the government's refusal during the entire time to recognize, officially at least, that the design was advanced and practical, and there was a waiting market. Even the engineering report to the trustees was kept under wraps until long after the trial.

John N. Kern, an attorney at the plant, lost only a few days when it was closed, going back to work on the trustees' payroll. Kern said he and another Tucker white collar man decided to find out for themselves how the car drove and what it was like.

"There was a straight gravel road inside the plant about a mile long," Kern recalled. "We put the Tucker against a Hudson, one of the hottest stock cars that year, and the Tucker beat it in every gear. We put it against other cars in clay up to the middle of the hub caps, and it was the Tucker that walked out.

"The first time you stepped on the gas in low you would scare the hell out of yourself. Sometimes we took other people along and first thing we knew we had a waiting list. So we decided everybody who worked there ought to drive the car at least once."

There were still about 300 people on the payroll, so they gassed up three Tuckers and lined up the people at one end of a mile and one-half course inside the plant grounds.

"There was one little guy with a Polish name they called

Joe,'' Kern said. ''Maybe Personnel knew his real name but nobody else did. When Joe got under the wheel he could just barely see over it, but he put it in first as he was told and stepped on it.

''He got up to fifty-five before somebody told him it was time to shift, and when he got past sixty he was having a little trouble. The car started to weave and one of his buddies in the back seat told him, 'Hey, Joe, take it easy!'

''When we got out Joe's buddy said, 'You know, that's the first time Joe ever drove a car.' ''

''That right?''

''Yup. But he said he always heard anybody could drive a Tucker, and he wanted to find out.''

There were not only plenty of Tucker cars, but millions of dollars in tooling and equipment, supplies and raw materials, most of which was sold later at junk prices. But with the evidence right under its nose, the government insisted throughout that the car was a fake and Tucker was a phony who never intended to build automobiles. The slander spread and multiplied, and Tucker was branded a fraud by people who wouldn't have known a butterfly valve from a spline shaft. One dealer commented at the time:

''A lot of jerks who never handled more than $6,000 or $7,000 a year in their lives suddenly knew exactly how $20,000,000 should have been spent.''

It is possible that the prolonged investigation by SEC and the FBI produced enough dirt on Tucker personally to make certain officials feel justified in knocking him off. But there was no possible justification—either legal or moral—for misrepresenting the Tucker automobile to achieve that end.

The government not only ignored evidence in its own possession, it disregarded the testimony of competent and experienced dealers across the country. Some of the basic principles of the Constitution are to guard citizens against injustice from their own government, and Tucker—whether innocent or guilty—was entitled to that protection.

Tucker's collapse started with the leak from SEC to Drew Pearson, and accelerated after the succeeding release of confidential information to the *Detroit News* and *Collier's*. Tucker people, after the *News* story, waited anxiously after the government announced it would investigate the source of the

News' "confidential" report. If the FBI expended one tenth
the energy checking the leak that it did finding out about the
backgrounds of Tucker's associates, the Justice Department
should have had the answer that same night.

The law was clear and specific regarding treatment of information obtained during investigations, and the Justice Department was bound—in theory at least—by the same laws
which governed SEC. And there could be no question whatever that both agencies considered the information secret and
confidential.

During the trial Assistant U.S. Attorney Lawrence Miller,
referring to documents he said would be made available to
the defense, told the court:

"But among these documents certainly is not the confidential report of the Securities and Exchange Commission. As
far as the reference to *Collier*'s and the *Detroit News* is concerned, why, we don't know anything about those newspapers, or where they got their information, if they got it."

Velie's deposition said he was given the report to read and
use in Kerner's offices in the Federal building, and in Hart's
office, where Hart furnished him office space and a desk.

A deposition taken from Martin S. Hayden, *Detroit News*
Washington correspondent, told a similar story of duplicity
and intrigue. Hayden said Harry A. McDonald, then Commissioner of SEC, gave him the report to read in a room at
the Statler Hotel in Washington.

McDonald, as Commissioner of SEC, could hardly plead
ignorance of the law, much less after two years in law school
at the University of Chicago. Yet he admitted giving the report to Hayden, in direct violation of the law, and later told
a Senate committee:

"My purpose was to protect the Commission against un-
justified criticism and to maintain public confidence in the
Commission. I would unhesitatingly do the same thing today
under similar circumstances."

But the pressure didn't stop with McDonald and Kerner.
Hayden's deposition said while SEC refused to let Tucker
even see the report, still insisting it was "confidential," he
got a copy from the Tucker trustees for *News* attorneys to use
in fighting Tucker's $3,000,000 libel suit. Asked why he went
to the trustees, Hayden explained:

"Well, I could not get the detail of it from the SEC, and I preferred not to cause Mr. McDonald any more trouble, and the trustees had it. I knew that. I talked with the Justice Department about it, and the Attorney General said he saw no great objection to my having the report, but there was a considerable problem as to how they were going to copy it in order to let me have a copy of it. It just seemed the easiest and most logical place to get it was from the trustees."

The government's part in the whole drama posed some interesting questions. Why wasn't the information on Hart and McDonald made public at the time? Was protecting McDonald's name and SEC's prestige more important than justice to Tucker and Tucker investors? And why was the government still supporting the *News* against Tucker, long after the trial was over?

Was there a conspiracy of silence that included even the Attorney General's office?

Whether the leaks came from SEC or Justice wasn't important. It was SEC's responsibility to keep its findings and opinions confidential and if the first leak was an accident or a mistake, the Commission could have made it right with a public statement. But it never did. The leaks which followed were in the same pattern, and again the government made no traceable effort to minimize their effect, or to expose the people who were responsible.

Tucker shot some fast angles and cut some corners, but there wasn't enough evidence to convince the jury that he was wantonly dishonest, or that he wasn't sincere in trying to produce automobiles. When the final score was in on both sides, about all it proved was that the opposition held the high cards. Careful study of the evidence points to only one conclusion: the government itself destroyed the corporation.

Trying to answer the question of what went wrong with Preston Tucker and his car isn't a simple matter of re-reading the script to separate the bad guys from the good guys. Because designing and producing an automobile isn't as simple as painting a picture or composing a symphony or raising hogs. The story becomes complicated because so many people are involved. Other companies and other industries. A variety of conflicting talents, personalities and interests which can never be merged into a smoothly operating whole, because the picture itself changes from day to day, even from hour to hour.

It isn't like taking some simple new product such as, say, a can opener to a company and saying: "Here, make this." No one man could ever get an automobile into production, no matter how gifted or how determined.

One of the early steps is analyzing the problems that others in the field have faced, and how they solved them. No one man knows the answers, whether in finance, production or sales. There must be limitless cooperation and innumerable advisers and experts. Some will be tremendously valuable, others will prove useless. When you start from scratch in a venture this size you have to get help where you can find it, with little or no guarantee of either competence or loyalty.

General Motors, greatest in the field, has lost millions when somebody goofed or conditions changed, even with many of its complex operations long since reduced to formulas. Like government, it has become so vast that no one man can even know its many activities, much less understand them. Every big corporation, including General Motors, has its bona fide experts and its phonies. Tucker, on a smaller scale, was no exception.

Starting with a new and simplified design may, from the outside, look relatively simple. But even the most carefully worked out designs will have to be worked over endlessly, as the many people and departments involved demand changes that are necessary for their purposes. Such changes may result from whim, with authority behind it. Others stem from real or imagined necessity, most often from purchasing, production and sales. The end result will inevitably be a compromise that will placate, if not satisfy, the many persons and departments involved. Even then the design cannot remain static, because progress is a continuous process and only progress can meet competition.

When Tucker crashed the automotive field he found a hostile industry that was solidly entrenched and wanted no interlopers poaching in its private preserve. The auto industry was long established, it had learned the rules of government, even helped to make them. So when a newcomer like Tucker entered the field with an ingenious and practical plan to raise capital, the government was there, ready to block him.

"You can't do it that way. You will have to do it this way."

There were other rules, hundreds, even thousands of rules, and the government was there ready to enforce every one of them. When a newcomer tries to cut corners he invites the law to land on his head.

Besides the opposition of powerful competitors and the constant harassment by government, there was the seething and ferment that is a part of any large organization. People inside and out who want to capture part or all of the operation and take it over. Plots and counter plots, ambition and intrigue. Angle for a raise. Undercut the boss and get his job. Sell out to the enemy and get a better job there. Dethrone the king and take over.

These, in ridiculously simplified form, were the problems that Preston Tucker faced when, on a comparative shoestring, he horned into one of the most savagely competitive fields in business today. It is a tribute to his ability and determination that he got as far as he did.

Who could have done any better under the circumstances?

The Price
of Progress

IT CAN BE ARGUED, WITH CONSIDERABLE LOGIC AND RATHER
convincing evidence, that the government delayed progress
in automotive design at least ten years when it put Tucker out
of business in 1948. If Tucker had continued, the industry
would have had to move with him and the public wouldn't
have waited this long for aluminum engines, and at least a
gesture toward economy of operation.

To the public, the Tucker trial was little more than a side-
show in which the real issues were obscured: whether risk
capital is a legitimate tool for attempting progress, or whether
in the future men can look solely to government, gambling
only on their ability to live long enough to collect Social
Security.

The important question is not whether the public suffered
by having to wait for aluminum engines, but whether the next
Tucker—whatever his name may be—will also have the odds
against him multiplied by the government itself.

It is inherent in long shots that the promoter will very possibly lose, and his investors along with him. But it might

seem that the least his backers deserve is the same chance to win or lose they would get at Hialeah. The government doesn't indict the owners of a track when a horse loses, or the operator of a casino when some citizen puts his last $50 on red and it comes up black.

It will sound like a pronouncement from the National Association of Manufacturers or the Union League, but it nevertheless is fact that courage and venture capital—just plain gamblers' guts—created every major asset this country has today, from oil and minerals to invention and industry. Not gambling for the petty returns from poker, slot machines and race tracks, but gambling for stakes that can affect the nation, or even the world.

Risk is the price of progress, and when risk is removed as an element of the American Economy, progress will eventually be limited to the work of captive scientists, in the narrow channels fixed by men whose chief concern is national power and prestige.

When the little men in SEC condemned Tucker as "having only a smattering of mechanical ability," it was more than willful distortion of facts. It was failure to realize— and admit—that men like Tucker were responsible for the industrial and technical superiority which kept this nation on top of the pile through two world wars and many decades of peace.

A handful of audacious and gifted men built the automotive industry in America, few of them inventors or even competent mechanics. But all were promoters who, like Tucker, risked their backers' money on dreams.

David D. Buick, one of the few who might have qualified as an inventor, died broke, and if the rest had depended on their own limited engineering ability they probably would have too. The greatest was William C. Durant, founder of General Motors. Durant was a salesman, as were Paul Hoffman of Studebaker and George Romney of American Motors. These were not detail men, but promoters—gambling against odds that make the casinos of LasVegas look like Bingo at a village street fair.

The Securities and Exchange Act of 1934 was conceived in a period of depression, when it wasn't a problem of balancing security against risk because few could afford risk, beyond an occasional penny ante game or a round with the slot machines. Sausage and hamburger sold as low as five cents a pound, and tens of thousands of persons had to look to the government or charity for even the five cents.

This legislation is already twenty-five years old, and while it may have served a useful purpose in its time, continued it will inevitably stifle new enterprise and with it progress, leaving the field—as with automobiles—to the few giants powerful enough to resist the unending assaults by an army of lawyers, bankrolled by the United States Treasury.

If the theory is accepted that Tucker's biggest mistake was bad timing, there can be no valid complaint over the government's action, or even the means that were used. Because it was no more than carrying out the will of the majority, preserving the status quo and its questionable security at the expense of progress.

But if the nation still believes in private enterprise, even if only in theory, the government's action must be deemed a mistake, which if continued may well prove tragic. An emasculated free enterprise system, by itself, will never be able to counter progress in vital new societies like Russia and China, and eventually India.

Tucker was by no means an isolated example of the Commission's zeal in protecting the public without worrying about the ultimate effect on all new enterprise. What set Tucker apart was the wide publicity the case received. And in spite of being technically a failure in the automotive field, he had become a legend long before his death.

If any morals are to be drawn from the Tucker story, one might be that if you want to promote something that needs more capital, go somewhere else and do it through foreign aid. Tucker dealers bellowed long and loud, though it didn't do them any good, when they discovered that while they were trying to reorganize the company the government dug up $40,000,000 for Fiat in Italy. Fiat is fast becoming one of the major competitors in the American small car market.

More important and deadly serious is the future of speculative investment—whether the Securities & Exchange Commission will continue its autocratic control over new business depending on risk capital, with life-and-death powers over business at the discretion of minor officials, their actions concealed in a blanket of secrecy that even the State Department might envy.

Present restrictions are stupid and dangerous, and SEC's endless tirades against gambling in securities are futile, because people are going to gamble in one way or another regardless of law. Under Prohibition it soon became apparent that people would go right on drinking. The only question was whether they would drink legally, and whether the profits would go to legitimate operators or to bootleggers and gangsters.

For the same reason, regulations governing securities should be re-evaluated so speculative issues can be sold and traded without their backers and investors being hamstrung by over-zealous bureaucrats, to whom even legitimate gambling seems to rank somewhere between sexual perversion and embezzlement. At least the profits could be channeled to some useful purpose, with always the possibility that something of real value could result.

Present practice in raising venture capital is to hire high-priced attorneys to find legal loopholes, which is expensive to everybody including the taxpayers, and benefits nobody but the lawyers. Relaxing the rules on risk capital could to a degree supplement taxes, by levying a percentage on speculative stock when it is sold, before there is even a question whether the investors will win or lose. It certainly would be as moral as selling Federal gambling stamps in Iowa, and using Federal agents to collect taxes where gambling is illegal.

It is highly unlikely, from SEC's past record, that anything short of legislation could alter its policies. If there is to be a change, the solution would seem to be corrective measures that will make a clear distinction between securities as covered under present laws, and those sold and described openly as speculative.

No better example can be found of the results of present SEC practices than Tucker Corporation, which wasn't broke when it went into trusteeship, had been under trustee ship more than ten years, had millions in assets yet has never paid a dime to its investors, who at least had a

227

long chance of winning as long as the company stayed in business.

The price of progress is risk, and when constructive risk can be re-established as a legitimate factor in new enterprise it may open a new era of industrial expansion. If the example of the Tin Goose could accomplish this and nothing more, it will have been well worth while.

_32_

The New Tucker

ALL THROUGH THE TRIAL TUCKER WAS PLANNING A COME-
back—trying to figure out designs and methods that would
avoid the mistakes made in the first round. He insisted
throughout that it was no disgrace, nor even unusual, to fail
in the automobile business. Ford and Durant both had failed
and come back to win; he would do the same.

I worked with Tucker once more beginning in May of 1952.
Some time earlier I had been with a Detroit advertising agency
that was backing Taft for president, and when the nomination
went to Eisenhower the agency lost interest. Tucker had been
asking me to come back with him, so I moved out from
Detroit and went to work.

The year before he had gone to Brazil with plans for an
entirely new car. He found people who would put up the
money, but only under the condition that he do the entire
development work there, which he refused to do. He still
might have worked something out if it hadn't been for the
timing; there was a presidential election coming up and the

people he was negotiating with were waiting to see how it came out.

Tucker's arrival at Galaeo airport, outside Rio de Janeiro, furnished unexpected entertainment for a crowd that was waiting when the plane came in. Other passengers included two high officials from the U.S. State Department, and the United States Ambassador to Brazil was there with his top aides. As reported by the *Chicago Tribune*, the Embassy delegation was all set when the Brazilian quarantine officer boarded the plane, ready for a ceremony that would impress the natives and bolster national prestige.

But it was Tucker the officer called for, and as the Embassy group waited, he was whisked through customs without even checking his luggage, accompanied by two unidentified but apparently influential Brazilians.

Tucker left Brazil without making a deal, but he arranged to keep in touch with potential backers until after the election, and said meanwhile he would try to develop the car himself in Ypsilanti.

In Ypsilanti the tool company had plenty of work, including sub-contracts for military equipment that were bringing in good profits. Some of the Chicago people were with him again, including Dan Leabu and Warren Rice, who developed the first automatic transmission and was working on an entirely new design.

To build up the shop and bring in more work, Tucker decided we needed a brochure—not to promote the automobile, but to sell the shop's facilities and bring in business. A brochure, as before, meant pictures and it was another budget job. One night he asked his wife to get out some 8 x 10 prints left over from the Chicago deal to see if there was anything usable. There was one excellent picture of Tucker, sitting behind a big desk with a distinguished-looking chap beside him.

"The picture's swell," someone commented, "but who the hell is this guy?"

Nobody knew. In about an hour Tucker came back with the photo and said smugly:

"I know who it is. That's the King of Denmark. He was a prince then."

Tucker was wrong, but not far off. The man who helped

230

sell the Ypsilanti Machine & Tool Company in the new brochure was Prince Carl Bernadotte of Sweden.

As the new automobile began to take form, about the only resemblances to the last 48s were the rear engine, independent suspension and the crash pad on the dash. A year after the trial Tucker had said that, in his opinion, the 48 was already obsolete, even though it would still outperform plenty of current models at the time.

With the market nearing saturation in the higher-price brackets, Tucker said there would be no point in trying to build the first Tucker even if it could be done. So he returned to his earlier concept of a low-cost car that would combine sports car performance with an all-around utility vehicle. When I started he already had spent several thousand dollars on preliminary development of a new four-cylinder opposed air-cooled engine, and had two men working on an entirely new automatic transmission. It is probable that during the year Tucker spent between $40,000 and $50,000 on the new design, including scale clay models, working drawings and prints, and patterns and castings.

People who were sold on the first Tucker always cherished the hope that there would be another Tucker car. To them the story ended when he died, so there is little point in describing the new design in any detail. Horsepower of the new engine was set for 130 and it should have given the car spectacular performance. With an entirely new body and chassis, the new job should have weighed around 2,000 pounds, which would have given it an impressive horsepower-to-weight ratio.

Tread was standard for operation off paved roads, and wheelbase was planned somewhere under the smallest American cars. It would have the same pop-out windshield, and for added safety a roll bar. Chrome trim was almost eliminated, and on one model the usual chromed bumpers were replaced by rubber extrusions which fitted into modified channels. Production cost would be low and replacement simple.

Tucker was still insisting on front fenders that turned with the wheels, but it was a minor factor in overall design. Most of us believed privately that they would shake off in the first thousand miles, but we conceded that the least Tucker rated was to find out for himself—after all, it was his money. As in Chicago, there would be plenty of time to talk him out of it later.

One passenger car design looked like a natural for Latin America, where much of the population depends entirely on taxis. This model used a split front seat similar to the Jeepster, but so arranged that it could be converted easily into a taxi with front seat passengers facing the rear. If performance and economy were anywhere near what was expected, Tucker said the Latin American taxi market alone should be good for a year's production. It would further provide the finest proving grounds any new automobile ever had, plus free demonstrations and advertising. For firsthand, authoritative information on any automobile, ask the hack jockey who drives one.

There was no reason to doubt that the new Tucker would perform even better than the 48s, but more important than either design or appearance were Tucker's plans for manufacture and sale. These looked as nearly foolproof as anything could be without actually trying them out. Under the plans there would be no big complicated sales organization, and no central factory as such.

Throughout the year work continued on design and drawings, and some patterns were made and a few castings. But when Tucker couldn't raise enough money to build a complete prototype he decided to close down until after the election in Brazil, and go back for another try.

It would have taken somewhere around $100,000 to build the kind of prototype Tucker wanted, and the shop wasn't making enough money to handle it. So just one year after I went to Ypsilanti he closed the plant except for a few small jobs, and rented out sections of the big building for income.

Tucker wasn't interested in just making money, beyond his immediate needs, if he couldn't build automobiles.

Could the Tucker be built today? The first Tuckers, the ill-fated 48s, are obsolete, even if the bugs were taken out and enough money could be raised to build them. But there is every reason to believe the new design could be built profitably under Tucker's detailed plans for manufacture and sales, and that the car would have even better performance and as great public acceptance as before.

33

The Game Is Over

THE YEAR SPENT TRYING TO GET THE NEW MODEL STARTED
in the Ypsilanti plant was the last time I worked actively with
Tucker, though I saw him frequently when I was around Detroit or we both happened to be in Chicago or New York. In
September of 1956 we planned to meet at Charlevoix, Michigan, but when I stopped at his mother's home I found nobody there. When I got back to Ypsilanti, Tucker said he had
been trying to reach me.

He had a big envelope with X-rays which he said three
hospitals had diagnosed as lung cancer, urging immediate
operation. (At the time he was still taking it easy after a
hernia operation some months earlier.) He knew I had had a
similar operation some years before and wanted to ask me
about it. I told him it was rough.

Tucker wasn't so much afraid of the operation as he was
doubtful that he could pull through another one so soon, and
doctors told him there was no time to lose. He was trying to
figure the odds, as a cousin in Grand Rapids had died the
same year after both surgery and radium treatment.

Next day he went to his office and telephoned Dr. William F. Koch, a friend of many years, whom Tucker had visited during his earlier trip to Brazil in 1951. Like Tucker, Koch was a controversial figure and the controversy had been continuing since the early 1940s, when he closed his cancer clinic and laboratory at Detroit after a long and bitter fight with the American Medical Association and the U.S. Food and Drug Administration. There was a further parallel in that Koch had been indicted, tried and freed in Federal court, but afterwards gave up and moved his laboratory to Rio after continuous investigation by Food and Drug agents. Tucker, remembering his own experience in Chicago, was understandably suspicious of the government's motives in the Koch case.

He wasn't convinced that Koch's treatment was a sure cure, but he thought the odds were at least as good as in surgery, and he had talked with a lot of people who said Koch cured them after other doctors had given them up. Tucker also was impressed with the doctor's background and many years of teaching, which included histology and embryology at the University of Michigan and physiology at Detroit Medical College.

He asked Koch to tell him which major medical centers in Europe were working on cancer, and then he called doctors in Heidelberg and London. He said they all told him they were no longer recommending surgery for his type of cancer, and warned him particularly against radium. He talked with doctors around Detroit, and said the best odds he could find for surgery were ten to one, and he thought they were too long, so he talked with Koch a few more times and made his decision: he would go to Rio and have Koch himself administer the treatment.

After he had made up his mind definitely, Tucker one night phoned his friend Max Garavito in New York, and asked him to get plane reservations. He told Max he had cancer and was going to Brazil for treatment. I couldn't hear Max's end of the conversation, but Tucker listened for a long time before he said good-bye to Max, adding that he would see him in New York.

"Emotional, isn't he?" Tucker said with a smile as he set the phone down.

In the week before he left, Tucker lived pretty much as he had before and said physically he felt fine. At Koch's direction he had stopped smoking and was eating only vegetables, and his only complaint was his diet: if Tucker didn't have meat, he wasn't eating. He kept business appointments in his office and went to a classic car meet at Grosse Pointe. One afternoon he went to get his Cadillac, which was being tuned up, and spent an hour helping mechanics tune up another Cadillac that was in for service. He assembled and arranged a lot of material on the new auto design, and said he would work on it after he got organized in Brazil.

If Tucker had buried any money after the Chicago deal he had run out now, because he had to borrow money to buy plane tickets for himself and Mrs. Tucker to Rio. They left in September.

When he saw the doctors he told them to hurry, he was losing time. He had a car to produce and he had to get to work on it. He was still working on designs for the "New Tucker."

First letters were hopeful and he had started another deal to build the automobile there. The election was over and one of the men he had been negotiating with before was back in Rio from temporary exile. This was multi-millionaire Adhemar de Barros, who entertained the Tuckers in his home while they were trying to get together on a deal.

"Mr. de Barros said they needed that type of automobile in Brazil and that he would get Preston all the money he needed," Mrs. Tucker said, "but he wouldn't send any money to the United States. He said they had all the facilities they needed at Sao Paulo, and they were still arguing about it when he came to see Preston at the hotel, after Dr. Koch said he had to stay in bed."

In October Tucker wrote that he was getting along all right, but complained about the climate and food.

"It's terrible here," he wrote. "Damp, cold, salty and humid."

He was depressed by the weather and his surroundings and decided to leave, planning at first to stop at Havana, where it would at least be warmer, but finally deciding to return directly to Ypsilanti. He was weak, having lost about fifty pounds, and Koch didn't want him to make the trip by air, warning that severe change in air pressure could stop improvement, or even reverse the effects of the treatment. But Tucker was determined, and left with his wife early in November. On the flight from Caracas to New York he had to have oxygen.

When he got home Tucker didn't look so bad except for having lost weight, and he was still yelling about the diet. At times he seemed to be better, but after having to have oxygen brought to the house several times he asked to be moved to the hospital, where he said they had good nurses and everything they needed to take care of him. By then he was down from 200 pounds to less than 100, and he refused to see anybody but the family and a few friends.

Before Tucker left Rio, Dr. Koch had prepared a schedule for Mrs. Tucker, telling her what symptoms to look for over the next months, what developments to expect in his condition—when to expect particularly rough times, and when breathing would become easier. The X-rays showed cancer only in the right lung, but Koch told the family later that his own diagnosis showed that the cancer had spread almost through his entire system. He had told Tucker what he was up against, but said Tucker asked him not to reveal his condition to any of the family.

A letter from Koch afterward said he was apprehensive when Tucker left, and that he believed he had suffered a hemorrhage in the infected lung from lowered pressure in the plane. The hemorrhage, Koch said, took too much of his breathing space so he couldn't get enough oxygen to support the recovery process. Like Koch, Mrs. Tucker said she couldn't blame her husband for wanting to come home, but she will always wonder whether the treatment might have worked if they had stayed.

"I honestly don't know whether Preston would have recovered or not, if we had stayed in Rio or Havana," she said.

"I do know that everything Dr. Koch told me came out exactly as he said it would, right to the day. Maybe if Preston hadn't been so set on coming home, and hadn't ridden all that distance in airplanes, he would have been better.

"Maybe there wasn't any hope from the start. But he was doing what he felt was best, and that was good enough for me."

About a week before Christmas I went to see Tucker at the hospital before leaving over the holidays. He was in an oxygen tent and he was tired, as another visitor had just left.

"For today, I've had it," he said.

I told him I would be back in a couple of weeks, when he could talk better.

"If I can't then, I'm not going to," he said.

A few days before Christmas the doctors said he had pneumonia. His mother said she had pulled him through pneumonia twice when he was a small boy, and she could do it again. She went to a drug store and bought vaseline and oil of peppermint. When she got back the doctor and a nurse were in the room, and the nurse started to protest.

"It's all right," the doctor said gently. "It can't hurt him."

His mother mixed a few drops of peppermint oil with vaseline and rubbed it on his back and shoulders, and he said he felt better and went to sleep. In a few hours he woke up and asked her to put more on.

He seemed to improve for a while, but he grew steadily weaker. Finally, at 4:55 o'clock in the afternoon, the day after Christmas, Preston Tucker died.

Controversy centered around Tucker almost up to his last hours. Pneumonia was reported to be the immediate cause of death, instead of cancer. It was rumored that tests which had been made showed that the cancerous condition had been arrested. When members of the family wanted to see reports on the tests, they said the hospital refused to tell them anything. One of his sons, one afternoon, took the chart from the foot of the bed into the men's washroom to read it, where he was reasonably sure the nurse wouldn't follow. He said the report showed a negative reaction to the tests.

Doctors in attendance said the report would be almost meaningless without a biopsy. No autopsy was performed, so the arguments continued. If the Koch treatment had cured, or even arrested the cancer, it hadn't saved his life, so nothing was proved one way or the other.

Just before the funeral I met Tucker's youngest son, who was going into the chapel.

"I'll bet Dad's laughing right now," Johnny said, "thinking what a man has to do to get you into a white shirt and a necktie."

He probably was, because it was an argument that had started long before the first deal moved from Ypsilanti to Chicago.

Tucker had made his last headlines, but he is remembered by a small group of men who worked with him in Chicago, trying to build a new automobile, and by a larger group throughout the world which hoped some day to drive it. To many of these people, Tucker had already taken his rightful place among the greats of automobile history, even before his death.

There is no object here of vindicating Tucker, who is beyond caring who was right and who was wrong. The automotive industry wrote his epitaph, as a true and discerning prophet in his narrow field, when it adopted—one after another—ideas he had announced and planned to use. Whether he was a hero or a fool wasn't important; he acted under compulsions which seemed beyond his control, and probably were beyond his understanding.

In a cemetery near Flat Rock, Michigan, there is a plain stone with a small bas-relief in bronze of the Tucker automobile, and somewhere in the record behind that figure is the story of what happened. If Tucker, and his stockholders and dealers, had been playing against a stacked deck, as many of them believed, the question of who stacked the deck was no longer important.

The game was over.

A thesis completed recently at the University of Michigan, by an engineer with almost a lifetime's association with the auto industry, predicts that within the next ten to fifteen years most American cars will have engines in the rear, like the Tucker. Stylists already have anticipated the change with simulated louvres and grilles.

If the prediction is right, the industry will have paid its final tribute to Preston Tucker.

Private Lives of Very Public People